THE CREATOR'S THREE DIMENSIONAL STRATEGIC PLAN AND PURPOSE FOR HUMANITY

THE 3RD DAY CHURCH.

Winston Lucien Daniels

*Our mission is to efficiently provide the world's finest, most comprehensive book publishing
service, enabling every author to experience success. To find out how to publish your book, your
way, and have it available worldwide, visit us online at www.trafford.com*

Trafford rev. 2/23/2010

Trafford
PUBLISHING®   www.trafford.com

North America & international
toll-free: 1 888 232 4444 (USA & Canada)
phone: 250 383 6864 ♦ fax: 812 355 4082

CONTENTS

ACKNOWLEDGMENTS:

I would like to extend a special Thank You and my deepest appreciation to my wife, *Yolande* and my two boys Jade and Caleb. Because of your love and support I can accomplish what I have never ever imagined.

Thank you to the House of Alpha and Omega International Ministries for their respect, loyalty, faithfulness and support in what I am called to be and do in this generation and to be released to minister to the nations.

Thank you also to my Executive Leadership team, who faithfully executed every inspired work and assignment we are called to accomplish in the places that God has ordained for us and for being such a tremendous blessing to the people that God has entrusted us with.

A sincere thank you to my beloved son in the Lord, Mario Williams, who has been the editor of this project. This project has revealed to me that you are connected with the content of my heart. Thanks Mario...

INTRODUCTION

This book was an absolute given. It is a book that wanted to be written, and so it was done purely by inspiration and a spontaneous flow of the life of God that has been building up in me over the many years of serving Him with all my heart and soul. My own life has been changed and transformed by the revelation and insight I am about to share with you. Because of what it has done in my life, it therefore implies that this information is potent with life changing powers and energies that have the potential to change your life from glory to glory, just as by the Spirit.

I have many times woken up with a chapter that was downloaded into my heart and mind during my sleep, and I would sit down and draw from the streams of living waters within me with such great ease, feeling tired only afterwards. This reminds me of what Jesus said to a person that was touching the hem of His garment. He said who touched me? This is simply because virtue went out of Him. **And the whole multitude sought to touch him: for there went virtue out of him, and healed them all** (Luke 6:19). My promise is this to you: There is virtue that will flow from the pages that you are about to read and you will be made whole in some aspects of your life. There were times that I was talking to a person, and I would get another chapter of the book while I was busy talking and then went home to draw it out. Jesus promised us that anyone that would believe on Him, as the scripture has said, out of his belly shall flow rivers of living waters. This living water is the life, virtue and power of God in us. Writing is one of the ways through which I release these living waters to heal the earth by healing God's people through sound life changing knowledge, valuable insight and understanding. In what specific way are you wired by God to tap into these living waters to release it into the earth? Think about it and make it your goal to release these waters more often. The earth is our inheritance; let's act responsibly by finding unique creative ways to fix it. **The heaven, even the heavens, is the LORD'S: but the earth hath He given to the children of men** (Psalm 115:16). The earth is waiting for the revealing of the sons of God (Romans 8: 21).

I believe I have matured to a good level to say that I have a fair idea of what life is really all about. I know how it feels like to fail terribly, to have absolutely no sense of hope for a future, and what it feels like to suffer lack and insufficiency in a big way. With this come deep feelings of abandonment, fear of failure, low sense of worth and identity, horrible feelings of inadequacy, and no sense of purpose and direction in life. Nonetheless, all the above mentioned has faded away as life unfolded in mysterious ways for me when I accepted Christ and began a new life journey. Christianity is a way of life, not a religion. It is about having a relationship with your Creator and allowing Him to restore you and to make you whole and complete to become what you are meant to be and to do what you are wired for. Our relationship with Him tends to restore all our other relationships.

This book has been designed to provide some practical insight and understanding about the ways of God, helping to make the process of life somewhat understandable and easier to travel, with having understanding has the potential to uphold a person in difficult times. **Discretion shall preserve thee, understanding shall keep thee** (Proverbs 2:11) No doubt about it – life is hard. Not accepting this reality makes life become harder. Accepting the fact that life is hard makes life become easy because this reality produces a readiness in us to take responsibility, which releases our personal power to make things happen when life is hard. Life also taught me that some things that seem to be hard are many times easy things that have been neglected. It is the little foxes that spoil the vines. We have to give each aspect of our lives a good amount of attention to get where want to go in life. Life treats everyone the same, whether you are a believer or an unbeliever, evil or good. **For the Father makes His sun to rise on the evil and on the good, and sends rain on the just and on the unjust** (Mat 5:45). We always get back whatever we send out into this world. The question is, what are you sending out daily? Just look around yourself and you will see an image of what you are sending out daily by way of thoughts, words, attitude, action and habits.

This three dimensional pattern of God will show you the tremendous power of three. Aligning yourself with this pattern will cause you to see the hand of God more often. It is the difference between Moses, who knew the ways of God, and the masses, that only saw the hand of God. Knowing the ways of God position us to move the hand of God and to make miracles become a natural part or aspect of our lives. **For who has known the mind of the Lord, that he may instruct him? However, we have the mind of Christ** (1Corinthians 2:16). Those who know the ways of God are influenced by His Spirit, which enables them to know the mind of the Lord. The mind of Christ is the view, feelings, and temper of Christ.

Chapter 1

SEEK TO UNDERSTAND THE WAYS OF THE FATHER.

I will never ever forget the night that the Lord woke me up in the very early morning and instructed me to write down a series of things pertaining to His three dimensional pattern. I wrote it down and I did not really know what to do with it. Can you imagine someone coming to you and give you a successful franchise pattern? That is exactly what the Lord gave me, but I did not know what to do with it. It was something that still needed to be unfolded for me to get a grip on it. It is written that a faithful man will abound in blessings. I have been faithful for many, many years and so my time has come to abound in the many blessings of the Lord, but I was still unaware that my time has come.

These three dimensional patterns that I wrote down came into play when I attended a Training School in Australia. Even the opportunity to go to Australia has been something that I stumbled into. And so it happened that this knowledge that the Lord gave me set me distinctively apart from all the other students that came from eight different nations. The man in command who was training us began to touch on this subject and I was well able to contribute to the lessons that he taught. The understanding I had was adding tremendous value to the school and so this man became very much drawn to me. This immediately opened up a ministry door for me in Australia.

He then asked me to minister at his church and this led to me getting invites from eight different nations all at once. This is how the Lord made me an international speaker. After all, this has been the fulfilment of a word that we received many years ago. At that time we could not imagine how it will ever happen. The Lord simply gave me a revelation that gave me favour that brought me into the International world. The revelation of the pattern of three gave me power over my limitations. He promised to take our ministry international and He made it happen in His own mysterious ways. For He who promises my friend, is also very able to perform what He promised us – the key is to endure your developmental process patiently. **And thus, having patiently endured, he obtained the promise** (Heb 6:15).

David was anointed King, but he went through a severe process before he stepped into what he was anointed for. The Bible says that he behaved himself wisely, which simply means he did not promote himself because he was anointed king. He waited on God. The key to our destiny is not the anointing – the anointing is meant for service. The key to our destiny is character – the anointing positions us to do service; doing service develops humility, selflessness, greatness and character in us, which sets us up to step into our destiny. But he that is greatest among you shall be your servant (Matt 23:11). The anointing says sweet nothing about us – it is the fruit of the spirit that speaks about the person. The anointing reveals the awesome burden removing, yoke destroying power of God. Bear ye one another's burdens, and so fulfill the law of Christ (Christ is the anointing) – Galatians 6:2.

Please posture yourself to come to grips and full understanding of the power of the three dimensional revelation concerning God's dealings with humanity. It has been very helpful to me and our congregation. It makes no sense not to know how God is working in our lives. A lack of knowledge about this most important area has caused many

Christians to stay stuck at the same place for many, many years. This has cast a bad reflection on the Church, because of a lack of growth and real evidence that the Lord is indeed a good God. It is not enough to tell people that God is good – our lives should reflect His goodness in all areas that pertain to our natural lives. We are called to be a true witness of the work that the Lord has done in us, and a witness is only real if there is tangible evidence of what we are talking about. A witness without evidence is a false witness. Acts 1: 8 does not say that we should do witnessing; it says we should be witnesses unto the Lord. Being deals with personhood and the promise is that we shall receive power to become a witness. It is the power of God that will change and transform us into a witness. We always did it the other way around; we go around doing witnessing without becoming a true witness. Sharing our faith with others should be an inspired action wherein God gives us a divine moment with a person. Witnessing without being inspired has caused many to reject the Lord.

WHAT IS THE REAL PURPOSE OF THE THREE-DIMENSIONAL DEALINGS OF GOD WITH MANKIND?

- To restore the fallen state of mankind.
- To nurture and cultivate the image and likeness of God in each human being in every nation, tribe and tongue.
- To restore our original God-given ability to rule and reign in life.
- To restore the years that the locust had eaten, the cankerworm, and the caterpillar, and the palmerworm.
- To fulfill God's ultimate dream, which is to have One Big family made up of all nations, tribes and tongues who shall not fear thee, O Lord, and glorify thy name? for Thou only art holy: for all nations shall come and worship before thee; for thy judgments are made manifest (Rev 15:4).
- To roll away the reproach of the world off from us.

- To bring each child of God into their wealthy place.
- To turn ashes into beauty.
- To empower the weak and the poor, so that they may say, "I am strong and rich because of what the Lord has done".
- To heal the brokenhearted; to deliver the captives; recovering of sight to the blind, and to set at liberty them that are bruised (Luke 4: 18).

GOD IS A THREE-DIMENSIONAL GOD

God is a three-dimensional God – God the Father, God the Son and God the Holy Spirit. We are also three-dimensional beings, because we were created in the image and likeness of God Himself (see Genesis 1: 27). We are spirit, soul and body, according to 1Thess 5: 23 **And the God of peace himself sanctify you wholly; and may your <u>spirit</u> and <u>soul</u> and <u>body</u> be preserved entire, without blame at the coming of our Lord Jesus Christ.** God is very determined that we should be preserved entirely, without blame at the coming of Jesus. Preserve means that God wants to keep your whole being (spirit, soul and body) free from fault. God wants each one of us to be whole and complete, lacking nothing in all three dimensions of our lives – spirit, soul and body.

God starts this work the day you receive Jesus Christ as your Saviour and Lord. Philippians 1: 6 says to us that we can be very confident that God who begun a good work in us will eventually finish this work until the day of Jesus Christ. The day of Jesus Christ is the day when you have become an accurate representation of who He is. **As He is, so are we in this world** (1John 4: 17b). This work that God is doing in us is a three-dimensional work. There are three dimensions in which He works in us, whilst a dimension consists of many levels. In other words, we are traveling levels within these dimensions as God works in us both to will and to do for His good pleasure. We get stuck in life within these levels when we do not co-operate with God through our disobedience – we are to be partakers and co-workers of what God is doing in our lives. God Almighty will not enforce Himself on us. He has given us the power to choose – you are a free-will human agent of God on the earth.

We can all continually go to new levels all the time when we obey God and therefore experience new things in God and in our natural lives if we co-work with God. The Israelites outstayed themselves in their wilderness dimension, because of their disobedience and stubbornness. They got stuck in the wilderness and continued to walk around the same old mountain seeing the same old sceneries. Being stuck produces terrible boredom and frustration. Become conscious when you are going through feelings of boredom and frustration – it is signs that you got stuck. Obedience of what God wants you to do is the only way to get unstuck.

The Israelites moved from level to level within the wilderness dimension by the pillar of the cloud by day and the pillar of fire by night every time when they obeyed the instructions that Moses gave them. This resulted in them seeing the hand of God working in their lives, which manifested in awesome mind-blowing miracles. It must have been very awesome to see the Red Sea paved into a wide street through which they could have walked on dry ground to get to the other side. One can only wonder what went through the minds of the Egyptians when they saw this.

The very same principle applies to us who are God's New Testament people. We get stuck when we do not co-operate and obey God. I know many Christians who served God for many years, but they got stuck in life – they are going nowhere. They have Jesus but they do not really enjoy life. That's a tragedy. How can you have the Prince of Life living in you, but yet not enjoying life? This is a good place to say that the Church is the most boring place on the earth if you do not do Church right. On the contrary, Church is the most exciting place on the earth if you do it right.

I one time had an experience that shocked me greatly. An unbeliever asked me this question: How is it that your ministry has excelled in such a short period of time in comparison to all the other Pastors that are struggling for so many years? How do you answer such a question about your very own born again brothers? I said to him I do not really know. But this is what I knew in my heart: Only those who are led by the Spirit of God are the true sons of God in this world. True sons of God are full grown sons and daughters of the Most High God – they excel in whatever they do, because they have learned how to co-work and partake in the work God is doing in them and in the world. **For as many as are led by the Spirit of God, they are the sons of God** (Romans 8:14). True sons of God continually move from glory to glory by the pillar of the cloud by day and the pillar of fire by night as they obey the now Word of the Lord, which is a proceeding Word from the throne of grace. **He that hath an ear, let him hear what the Spirit saith unto the churches** (Rev 2:11).

These three-dimensional works can clearly be seen operating in the lives of the Israelites, because the natural reveals the spiritual. They were the Old Testament people of God and experienced God's three-dimensional dealings naturally, whereas we experience this three-dimensional developmental process spiritually. **Howbeit that *was* not first which is spiritual, but that which is natural; and afterward that which is spiritual** (1Corintians 15:46). We are born as natural human-beings; therefore we need to be born again to become spiritual-beings. Sin has killed the spirit of man, but by receiving Christ our spirit-man comes alive. God is Spirit; therefore we can only come to Him via our spirit and through the Holy Spirit. **That which is born of the flesh is flesh; and that which is born of the Spirit is spirit** (John 3:6).

2Corithians 13: 1 confirms to us the power of three by saying that any matter gets established by two or three witnesses. Two witnesses are accepted if there are only two evidences to establish the matter, but three is a more powerful witness. The three-dimensions that this book is dealing with show us how God goes about to establish us and to make us stable and rock solid, like mount Zion that cannot be moved. **They that trust in the LORD shall be as mount Zion, which cannot be removed, but abides for ever** (Psalm 125:1). Beautiful for situation, the joy of the whole earth, is mount Zion, on the sides of the north, the city of the great King (Psalm 48:2).

So we read an account in Acts 10 of the vision that Peter saw as he fell into a trance and how he wrestled with what God showed him in the vision. God wanted to visit the Gentile world, because He wanted to adopt them into His royal family, but this was something contrary to Peter's doctrine. So God did it three times to convince Peter and to establish the matter in his heart and mind. **This was done thrice: and the vessel was received up again into heaven** (Acts 10:16). Three times this was done, doubtless to impress it on the mind of Peter with the certainty and importance of the vision. God does the same thing in our lives to establish His perfect will in our lives. There are three dimensions concerning the will of God to ultimately bring us into the perfect will of God for our lives. Romans 12: 2 clearly define these three dimensions of the will of God. Each of these dimensions consists of levels that we travel.

THE WILL OF GOD IS…
1. Good
2. Acceptable
3. And perfect.

This is just one example of this three dimensional process that we are all subjected to for God to, establish us in all areas that pertain to our lives.

Chapter 2

GOD'S DEALINGS WITH HUMANITY ARE THREE-DIMENSIONAL.

The spiritual meaning of three is establishment, completion or conclusion. We read in 2Co 13: 1 and Matthew 18: 16 that any matter gets established by the mouth of two or three witnesses. In this instance, we will specifically deal with witnesses of three. God who started a good work in our lives will finish it in the third Day, which we will explain in greater detail as we go deeper into this knowledge of the three days. **And He (Jesus) said unto them, Go ye, and tell that fox, Behold, I cast out devils, and I do cures to day and to morrow, and the Third DAY I shall be perfected** (Luke 13:32). Also keep in mind that one day equal "a thousand years" according to the writing of Peter. **But, beloved, be not ignorant of this one thing, that one day *is* with the Lord as a thousand years, and a thousand years as one day** (2Peter 3:8). These three days or three thousand years is God's divine schedule, plan and purpose for humanity, which are so dear to His heart.

Well, I studied Production Management and Industrial Engineering and I was also actively involved in Process Engineering. This has been my training grounds to learn and understand the depth and wonder of the power of a process. I am so grateful for this kind of life experiences that I gained in the automobile industry, because it inspired me to buy into Process, which most of us tends to dislike. We all want what we want now, but unfortunately that is not how life works, as life itself is a process–an ever unfolding mystery. Anything that gets produced follows this pattern: **Input – Process – Output** (finished product). We are God's created beings and have been designed to be fruitful, to multiply, to replenish the earth, to subdue it and have dominion; yet the truth of the matter is that we have lost the capacity and ability to do what we have been created for, because of the destructive powers of sin, caused by the disobedience of Adam and Eve. This has created the need for restoration to make us whole and complete.

Our lives are therefore subjected to **Input – Process – Output** and this is what the pattern of three is all about. All of my life experiences have set me up to write this book. I have personally witnessed the pattern of three in my life, my marriage and in whatever I am doing in life.

LET'S NOW LOOK AND SEE WHAT THE LORD DID IN EACH DAY

And He (Jesus) said unto them, Go ye, and tell that fox, Behold, I cast out devils, and I do cures to day and to morrow, and the Third DAY I shall be perfected (Luke 13:32).

1. Today (first day) is the day in which He cast out devils
2. Tomorrow (second day) is the day in which He does **all cures**
3. Third day is the day that the Lord will perfect His work.

We clearly see in the Old Testament that these three dimensions for the Israelites were **Egypt**, the **Wilderness** and the **Promised Land**. God started His work in them in the land of Egypt when He assigned Moses to set the people free from the oppressive leadership of Pharaoh. Moses came to them in Egypt with a divine assignment and a promise from God. The promise was that God would make these oppressed people a peculiar treasure unto Himself, a people above all people's in the earth. They would no longer have to toil, labour and sweat to make a mere living. Instead, He would give them a land that flows with milk and honey, houses that they did not build and vineyards that they did not plant. This most probably sounded ridiculous for an oppressed person to be called a treasure and a special person above all people. Good news upsets oppressed people, because it contradicts all of their human experiences. Can you imagine all the doubt and unbelief that these people struggled with that Moses had to deal with? It is also a very hard thing for an oppressed person to receive the messenger of good news or anything that sounds too good to be true. Good news is very much confrontational in a soul that only knows the bad side of life. No wonder they say that **only** bad news sell in the newspaper industry.

Nevertheless, God started His miraculous work in His people in Egypt, and He brought them out with an outstretched arm, and with great terribleness, and with signs, and with wonders. God was good to them, but the good news is that God is much better to us, because we received a better covenant than them. The truth of the matter is, His first works are the greatest miracle in our lives. This miracle is a transition out of the kingdom of darkness into His wonderful kingdom. Yet, it does not feel so when we undergo His second work in the second dimension, which is the wilderness. Yet God was faithful to bring them out of the wilderness into the Promised Land, except those who did not believe the promise. Things get done unto us according to our faith, because faith is the only thing that pleases God. **Even so, without faith it is impossible to please him: for he that cometh to God must believe that he is, and that he is a rewarder of them that diligently seek him** (Heb 11:6). Their unbelief led them to disobey the Lord their God. Thus, obedience determines our destiny. The Lord did enlarge their coast, as He had sworn unto their fathers, and gave them all the land which He promised to give unto their fathers. Nonetheless, only those who believed and obeyed Him could enter His rest for them. There remain a rest for us… don't miss out!

This is the conclusion of the matter: God's Old Testament people (Israelites) could not be made perfect without us (New Testament people), because God has provided better things for us. **And these all, having obtained a good report through faith, received not the promise: God having provided some better thing for us, that they without us should not be made perfect** (Heb 11:39-40). Even though they have entered into the Promised Land, they were unable to maintain their place in the Promised Land, because the power of sin was not yet destroyed. Jesus came and destroyed the power of sin, so that we could be made perfect. **For this purpose, the Son of God was manifested, that he might destroy the works of the devil** (1John 3:8b). The devil destroyed their Promised Land because the Son of God was not yet manifested to destroy his evil work against them. Therefore, there still remains a rest for us, because God's promise of a rest for His people must come to perfection. Remember the words of Jesus recorded in Luke 13: 32 – Tell that fox that I will perfect My work on the 3rd Day.

In the same way, we can also not be made perfect without them (Israelites). They have provided for us a natural blue print of the plan and purpose of God, because the natural comes before the spiritual. The natural can be seen, whilst the spiritual is the unseen. We who are the spiritual people of God can now see beyond the unseen by looking at their natural example. We are to praise God for this – even though we deal with an unseen world (unmanifested), we are now more than able to have practical insight into unseen realities because of the pattern they have provided for us.

GOD'S DEALING WITH HIS NEW TESTAMENT PEOPLE

We now understand according to Hebrew 11: 39-40 that both the Israelites and we cannot be made perfect without each other. It therefore makes perfect sense why Paul said that God has not cast away His people (Jews) which He foreknew. The only purpose why we have received better promises is to make all of us perfect. **For by one Spirit are we all baptized into one body, whether we be Jews or Gentiles, whether we be bond or free; and have been all made to drink into one Spirit** (1Cor 12:13). The truth of the matter is that we are all one in Christ. We are not better, neither are the Jews any better – we are all one in Christ. **Is He the God of the Jews only? Is He not also of the Gentiles? Yes, of the Gentiles also** (Rom 3:29).

Our Egypt is the world and the Babylonian system that kept us in bondage – we were slaves to sin, just like the Israelites were the slaves in Egypt under the oppressive leadership of Pharaoh, who is a type of the devil. **Jesus answered them, Verily, verily, I say unto you, whosoever commits sin is the servant (slave) of sin** (John 8:34). It is Jesus who bought us by the slave markets; He became a ransom price for our sin. **For ye are bought with a price: therefore, glorify God in your body, and in your spirit, which are God's** (1Co 6:20). This price was not gold or silver, but the precious blood of Jesus Christ our Savior. By Him paying this precious price for our sins we were translated out of the kingdom of darkness into His marvellous kingdom. The precious blood He shed on the cross spoilt principalities and powers and made a public spectacle of them by leading them as captives in His victory procession. These are such wonderful words to utter – the devil and his foes were defeated permanently – their only purpose for now is to train our hands to make war so that our arms can bend a bow of bronze. All kings send their kids to the army for training to get them ready for the throne. Keeping in mind that Jesus Christ washed us in His own blood and has made us **kings** and **priests** unto God and His Father; to Him *be* glory and dominion for ever and ever (Revelation 1:6).

This three-dimensional dealing of God started in Egypt, which is the world for us. The world is where we have been delivered from. **Who hath delivered us from the power of darkness (world), and hath translated *us* into the kingdom of His dear Son** (Col 1:13). With a mighty outstretched arm the Lord delivered the Israelites and brought them into the Wilderness, which is the Church dimension for us. We will draw lessons from the Israelites during their stay in the Wilderness in the next chapter. Everything they went through was written for our learning to make our journey out of the Church into the kingdom of God, which was their Promised Land, a manageable journey. It is always best to learn from other people's mistakes instead of making the same mistakes. **For whatsoever things were written aforetime were written for our learning, that we through patience and comfort of the scriptures might have hope** (Rom 15:4). The Old Testament is useful for us to illustrate to us God's dealings with His Old Testament people. We develop patience by enduring all the sufferings and hardship in the Wilderness dimension. Patience produces hope, according to Romans 5: 4, and hope does not disappoint.

THIS IS HOW HOPE UPHOLDS US DURING DIFFICULT TIMES.

- It inspires us that afflictions may prove to be a great blessing.
- That their proper tendency is to produce "hope."
- That the way to find support during affliction is to go to the Bible.

So many, of us have misrelated to the Church which has made Church an unpleasant experience for many of us. The Church is all about getting us ready to live a good life in the Kingdom of God on earth in the here and the now. Getting ready has hardship in it, yet hardship can be easily handled when we accept it as a natural part of the process of becoming. **If thou faint in the day of adversity,**

thy strength is small (Proverbs 24:10). This is how the Good News Bible puts it: **If you are weak in a crisis, you are weak indeed.**

CHAPTER 3

THE CHURCH IN THE WILDERNESS

Everything written long ago was written to teach us so that we would have confidence through the endurance and encouragement which the Scriptures give us - Romans 15:4.

I am fully convinced that many of us do not like the idea or the concept that the Church represents the wilderness. God Almighty wants to comfort us and give us hope through the scriptures and the power of the Holy Spirit. Jesus Himself has been in the wilderness for forty days to pave the way for us. Forty stands for a generation, which is to say that Jesus was paving a way for a generation to come. Wilderness tends itself to be a negative word as we associate pain to this word. Nevertheless, the Israelites have been the first people in the human race that has been "called out" from the world (Egypt). This is what Acts 7: 38 says about the Church being the Wilderness - **This is he that was in the church in the wilderness with the angel which spake to him in the mount Sina, and with our fathers: who received the lively oracles to give unto us?** The word "church" literally means "those called out," and often means an assembly or congregation. It is applied to Christians as being "called out" from the world. It also means the whole body of believers.

The wilderness is a hard-place, no doubt about it. We can only properly process things, events and circumstances when we are willing to face reality. This explains why there seem to be so many issues in the Church. The Church is a hard place. Trouble, issues, problems and negativity are the natural state of the wilderness and through a lack of understanding we have made so many wrong conclusions concerning the Church. I have many times heard this statement: The Church is the place where people get the most hurt. We tend to overlook the fact that "offences will come" is a promise, just like blessings, peace, prosperity, etc. are divine promises. God was using the wilderness to clean up His people from all their negativity and issues they accumulated in the Land of Egypt. An event that offends you has come to show you that you have issues in your tissues. Most of us desperately need shakings and shock therapy situations to unlock our old negative energies that are locked up in our tissues.

Moses really had the capacity and the grace to deal with all the negativity of the Israelites. In the same way Pastors should develop capacity to deal and work with the negativity of the people. Have you ever seen how the sea cleanses itself, with the seashore revealing the dirt that was in the sea? And so also do negative events, situations, and circumstances reveal the dirt that was in the people. It is always best for the dirt to come out of the people rather than being in the people. We should therefore encourage the people to move on without having to feel condemned or guilty about what came out of them. Some people's issues got real deep into their tissues so it will take some real intense pressure for these issues to surface to the forefront. The wilderness (Church) should be a safe place where people can be delivered from their issues and be supported by loving caring people. **Where no oxen (church people) are, the crib (church) is clean: but much increase is by the strength of the ox** (Proverbs 14:4). A church that increases in membership can expect the crib to become dirty. The Church is not a social club where everything is to be nice and clean to impress the elite. The truth is: there are many messed up people in very nice places because we refuse to apply the strength of the ox to clean up our people. We tend to prefer nice setting over people. God Almighty is too BIG to get worked up or upset about our flaws, weaknesses and shortcomings; instead He is willing to suffer long, to be merciful and to be good to us. His goodness and conviction always leads us to repentance every time when we miss the mark, bringing us in alignment with His ways of doing things. We should learn to be easy with people while we continually and graciously do our best to lift up their moral standards bit by bit, line upon line, here a little there a little, working with them through their flaws and shortcomings.

We will now carefully look into the life experiences of the Israelites in the Wilderness (the Church in the wilderness) and see how they have been cleansed from their issues. These people had terrible issues which were mixed with much ungratefulness. It is for this reason why we have introduced the gratitude journal concept in our ministry, because it becomes a little easier to work with people's issues if they at least have a sense of gratitude. God delivered the Israelites out of the hands of the Egyptians by paving open the Red sea in front of their very eyes and caused them to walk on dry ground, drowning their enemies whom they feared terribly. One would think that this would be a kind of miracle that they would never forget; yet three days after this awesome event they became negative and complained about the fact that there was no water to drink.

A grateful person would make a heartfelt connection that the same God who made a roadway through the Red Sea also has the power to provide water in the desert. Well, God did this by providing them water from a Rock. This was to proof to them that anything was possible with God. **Jesus said unto us, If you can believe, all things are possible to us that believes** (Mark 9:23)**.** How many believers have witnessed miracles, signs and wonders and yet when they are faced with a difficult situation, they tend to become negative and complaining. Studying the reality that the Church is the Wilderness has become so much clearer to me when I saw similarities between believers in the Church and the Israelites in the Wilderness. Studying the behavior patterns of the Israelites and making a connection of how badly they have treated Moses and God can really frustrate a person, which brings out the prejudice in us. Unbelieving, ungrateful believers have the exact same effect on us.

There were two Church splits in the Wilderness – rebellious leaders stood up against Moses and influenced some of the people negatively to turn against Moses and Aaron. This does not look any different than what is happening in the Church in today's age. Many Churches are born of rebellion, and they are producing after their own kind more and more rebellious believers that do the same thing. We impart who we are not what we know. Disrespect towards God's ordained leaders in the Church is as common as it was with the Israelites in the Wilderness. I trust that by now you can see that the Church is the Wilderness dimension. The world will not take us serious as long as we stay in the Wilderness dimension. Wilderness means: a natural uncultivated land; a mostly uninhabited area of land in its natural uncultivated state, sometimes deliberately preserved like this, e.g. a forest or mountainous region; barren area: an area that is empty or barren in the vast wilderness of outer space. This is what the Wilderness means within our context: uncomfortable situation - a place, situation, or multitude of people or things that makes somebody feel confused, overwhelmed, or desolate; the wilderness of the big city.

Let me also say this for the sake of balance: Church life is not only unpleasant although it is a wilderness. It is ultimately our obedience that determines our happiness in the wilderness. Every believer that fellowship in a ministry that really has the life of God in it have a history of good and terribly bad times concerning Church. Life in the Wilderness for the Israelites was pleasant when they obeyed the Lord, following the cloud by day and the pillar of fire by night. Trouble and unpleasantness broke out whenever they disobeyed and camped too long at one place. We can also see that much of the unpleasantness and suffering began to wear off the closer they got to the Promised Land. Let me say again, the Wilderness is a dimension and there are many levels within a dimension. Every new move of God is another level up higher, and it makes Church-life more pleasant and enjoyable for a season until we reach another ceiling. Yet, many ministries are missing out on what God is doing simply because they are attached to the last move of God and has labelled themselves with that specific move. We mistakenly label ourselves Pentecostal, Charismatic, Evangelicals, etc. – that's not who we are. We are God's kids, kings and priests unto God and our Father. It is heartbreaking that we have limited ourselves to these labels that have created so much division among God's people. All these labels keep us from moving on with the cloud. I will talk more about this in another chapter.

GOD IS THE ONE WHO TOOK THEM INTO THE WILDERNESS

- Who create the wilderness or circumstance? Answer - God
- Who set them up to be in the circumstance in their lives? Answer - God
- Who led Jesus into the wilderness? Answer - the Spirit of God (Matt 4: 1)
- Wilderness equals circumstance.
- Conclusion: God was responsible for the circumstance / wilderness.

Have you ever been led into a circumstance by God, and once you are in the circumstance things do not turn out the way you thought it would? Then you begin to question God by saying that you maybe did not hear God correctly or something like that. "I mean God would never lead me into trouble, He is the God of salvation". God is good all the time and all the time God is good. Have we as believers related correctly to the purpose and process of the Church in our lives? Well, I don't think so because so many of us got stuck in the Wilderness dimension whilst some of us are enjoying kingdom life on earth in a crazy world. It is foolishness to wait for the kingdom to come while you are stuck in the Wilderness – there is already a great dimension of the kingdom that has already come that can be enjoyed in the here and now. It is Jesus that said that the kingdom is at hand – it is right here for those who have repented (changed the way they used to think) and has believed the good-news of the message of the kingdom of God.

The purpose of the Wilderness was to produce character in them. God is more concerned about our character than our comfort and happiness. If you have character you can make yourself happy. God wanted to produce a special kind of people that stood out among the rest of the nations, whom others would be able to see and identify as the people of God. This desire and intention of God has not changed. In fact, He has fulfilled this purpose in Jesus Christ, who is the fullness of God's plan and purpose for humanity.

During the wilderness process God is the one that allowed negative, challenging, uncomfortable, high-pressure circumstances to confront them and us in the Church, which purpose it is to humble us and to test us and to see whether or not we would obey him. **And thou shall remember all the way which the LORD thy God led thee these forty years in the wilderness, to humble thee, and to prove thee, to know what was in thine heart, whether you would keep his commandments, or not. And he humbled you, and suffered you to hunger, and fed you with manna, which you know not, neither did their fathers know; that he might make you know that man doth not live by bread only, but by every word that proceeds out of the mouth of the LORD doth man live** (Deut 8:2-3).

THE PURPOSE OF THE WILDERNESS (DEUT 8: 2-3)

- To humble them, because it is the meek that will inherit the earth. They could not possess the Promised Land, unless they were humble.

- To prove them or put them to test.
- To show them what was in their hearts – He knows what is in our hearts.
- To see whether they would keep His commandments or not.
- He allowed them to suffer hunger, because a hungry tummy reveals the issues that are in your heart.
- He wanted them to make a heartfelt connection that man shall not live by bread alone but by every word that proceeds out of the mouth of the Lord.

All the above mentioned is what the Lord is doing in the Church right now, and, unless we make this connection, we too will die in the Church dimension and never enjoy kingdom life on earth before the coming of the Son of God. This is mirrored in the fact that most of the Israelites could not enter the Promised Land - **So we see that they (Israelites) could not enter in because of unbelief** (Hebrews 3:19). Do not be deceived, God is not mocked; He remains the same yesterday, today and forever. We will reap what we sow, even though the New Covenant is better than the Old one. We should never play around with the grace message to provide us an excuse to live below God's standards.

There was a shorter route to the destination; however, God led them on a longer route because He had a work to do in them. He did not want them to take their issues into the Promised Land and make their inheritance to become just like Egypt. **When Pharaoh let the people go, God didn't lead them on the road through Philistine territory, although that was the shortest route. God said, "If they see that they have to fight a war, they may change their minds and go back to Egypt." So God led the people around the other way, on the road through the desert toward the Red Sea. The Israelites were ready for battle when they left Egypt** (Exodus 13:17-18). The journey in the wilderness lasted 40 years. The book of Exodus has 40 chapters; 40 in Bible numeric stand for a generation.

In the wilderness, you will eat **what** God gives you to eat and **when** God wants you to eat and drink. God gives you food & drink that you are not used to and in our human nature, we tend to long back to what we had in the world (Egypt). All your friends go to the restaurants where you long to go eat, but you never have enough money to go eat at those restaurants. You have a certain type of clothing that you long to wear, but you do not have enough money to buy what you want. You don't have money to drive the kind of car you long to drive. You are tempted to say what David said to God: **Behold, these are the ungodly, who prosper in the world; they increase in riches. Verily, I have cleansed my heart in vain, and washed my hands in innocence. For all the day long have I been plagued, and chastened every morning** (Psalm 73:12-14). This scripture verse is the language of a good man perplexed and embarrassed by the fact that the wicked are prosperous and happy. The wicked people live regardless of God, and yet they are peaceful, tranquil, happy, and prosperous. The most disempowered word is called "unfairness", because immediately you relate to your circumstances in the fashion of giving away your power to the circumstance or the people whom you perceive to get more than what they deserve. This is based on comparison and the proverb reads "it is unwise to compare" as it more often than not leave your heart sick. Your biggest mistake is to bless yourself by buying on credit the things that you cannot afford. Don't do it! You will prolong your stay in the Wilderness. Allow God to strengthen your character through these heavy restrictions and limitations that the wilderness puts on you.

THE STRATEGIC LESSONS OF THE WILDERNESS

- **God was with them and the One leading them** -By day the LORD went ahead of them in a column of smoke to lead them on their way. By night he went ahead of them in a column of fire to give them light so that they could travel by day and by night. The column of smoke was always in front of the people during the day. The column of fire was always there at night - Exodus 13:21-22.

- **God fought on their behalf and supernaturally destroyed their enemies and delivered them from certain death** - The Egyptians pursued the Israelites. Pharaoh's army, including all his horse-drawn chariots and cavalry, caught up with them as they were setting up their camp by the sea at Pi Hahiroth facing north. As Pharaoh approached, the Israelites looked up and saw that the Egyptians were coming after them. Terrified, the Israelites cried out to the LORD. They said to Moses, "Did you bring us out into the desert to die because there were no graves in Egypt? Look what you've done by bringing us out of Egypt! Didn't we tell you in Egypt, 'Leave us alone! Let us go on serving the Egyptians'? It would have been better for us to serve the Egyptians than to die in the desert!" Moses answered the people, "Don't be afraid! Stand still, and see what the LORD will do to save you today. You will never see these Egyptians again – Exodus 14: 9-13.

- **God expects obedience to Him in exchange for healing and divine protection** - Moses led Israel away from the Red Sea into the desert of Shur. For three days they traveled in the desert without finding water. When they came to Marah, they couldn't drink the water because it tasted bitter. That's why the place was called Marah [Bitter Place]. The people complained about Moses by asking, "What are we supposed to drink?" Moses cried out to the LORD, and the LORD showed him a piece of wood. He threw it into the water, and the water became sweet. There the LORD set down laws and rules for them to live by, and there he tested them. He said, "If you will listen carefully to the LORD your God and do what he considers right, if you pay attention to his commands and obey all his laws, I will never make you suffer any of the diseases I made the Egyptians suffer, because I am the LORD, who heals you." Next, they went to Elim, where there were 12 springs and 70 palm trees. They camped there by the water - Exodus 15:22-27.

- **God allows them to hunger and gives them food with specific instructions to test their obedience.** The whole community of Israelites moved from Elim and came to the desert of Sin, which is between Elim and Sinai. This was on the fifteenth day of the second month after they had left Egypt. In the desert the whole community complained about Moses and Aaron. The Israelites said to them, "If only the LORD had let us die in Egypt! There we sat by our pots of meat and ate all the food we wanted! You brought us out into this desert to let us all starve to death!" The LORD said to Moses, "I'm going to send you food from heaven like rain. Each day the people should go out and gather only what they need for that day. In this way I will test them to see whether or not they will follow my instructions (Exodus 16:1-4). The Israelites ate manna for 40 years until they came to a place to settle. They ate manna until they came to the border of Canaan - Exodus 16:35

- **The people complain about water, yet God fights with them in battle to overcome their enemy**. The whole community of Israelites left the desert of Sin and traveled from place to place as the LORD commanded them. They camped at Rephidim, but there was no water for the people to drink. So they complained to Moses by saying, "Give us water to drink!" Moses said to them, "Why are you complaining to me? Why are you testing the LORD?" But the people were thirsty for water there. They complained to Moses and asked, "Why did you bring us out of Egypt? Was it to make us, our children, and our livestock die of thirst?" - Exodus 17:1-3

- **God begins to organize them into a civil community and gives Moses wisdom on how to rule the people well.** Now listen to me, and I'll give you some advice. May God be with you! You must be the people's representative to

God and bring their disagreements to him. You must instruct them in the laws and the teachings, show them how to live, and tell them what to do. "But choose capable men from all the people, men who fear God, men you can trust, men who hate corruption. Put them in charge of groups of 1,000, or 100, or 50, or 10 people. Let them be the ones who usually settle disagreements among the people. They should bring all important cases to you, but they should settle all minor cases themselves. Make it easier for yourself by letting them help you - Exodus 18:19-22. **A sure sign that your days in the wilderness are numbered is the day when there is order, structure, organization, management and leadership in place in your life.**

- **God prepares the people to reveal His covenant with them.** Then Moses went up the mountain to God, and the LORD called to him from the mountain, "This is what you must say to the descendants of Jacob. Tell the Israelites, 'You have seen for yourselves what I did to Egypt and how I carried you on eagle's wings and brought you to my mountain. If you carefully obey me and are faithful to the terms of my promise, then out of all the nations you will be my own special possession, even though the whole world is mine. You will be my kingdom of priests and my holy nation.' These are the words you must speak to the Israelites." (Exodus 19:3-6).

- **God established His covenant with them and gave them the Ten Commandments** (Exodus 20).

- **God gives them the laws that should govern their interrelationships** (Exodus 21 – 24).

- **God gives the instructions to build the tabernacle so that He could come to His people, to live and dwell among them** (Exodus 25 – 31).

GOD'S STANDARDS:

The LORD spoke to Moses, "Tell the Israelites: I am the LORD your God. You used to live in Egypt. Don't live the way the Egyptians do. I am bringing you to Canaan. Don't live the way the Canaanites do. Never live by their standards. Follow my rules, and live by my standards. I am the LORD your God. Live by my standards, and obey my rules. You will have life through them. I am the LORD - Lev 18:1-5. **How would you translate the above mentioned words into words that God would say to His New Testament people before they would make their transition from a Church dimension into a Kingdom Dimension, which is the 3rd Day Church?**

We are always restricted to go to the next level when we do not know where we are in the process. It is my sincere desire that you should locate yourself as to where you are and what are the things you have to work through to move to your next level in the wilderness, and ultimately to get out of the wilderness dimension. It is always a blessed thing to read an in-season book that speaks into your life. I trust that this is an in-season book for you. If not, make time to read it again when it feels in-season. It has been said that the teacher always appears when the student is completely ready.

Chapter 4

WHAT IT TAKES TO COME OUT OF THE WILDERNESS.

I think it is very important for us to upgrade our thinking concerning Church. We are not having Church because it is the right thing to do, or it is something that eases people's conscience that they have been in Church on Sunday. Church is something that is happening to us. We have learnt thus far that it was God that came up with the idea of a Wilderness – it is God's idea to set us up in what we call Church or the wilderness. He sets us up because He has a restoration work to do in us. We need the Church because we have issues that limit us, weaknesses, shortcomings, stuff that hinders us, unresolved matters that restrict us, unfinished business, things that intimidate us, sabotage us and make us fearful, and so forth. The wilderness has been designed to free us from all these things, so that we might become what we are born to be and do, which leads to having the things that we need, want and desire. We should therefore, relate to the Church as a discovery journey as we travel to get to the city which has foundations, whose builder and maker *are* God. This city is a kingdom of God reality on earth, which is more real than the people that you can see with your eyes. We have to stop being so churchy, for going to Church cannot and will not change the world – evidence and confirmation hereof is the fact that we have been attending "church" for many centuries, and yet it seems the world is worse off than before. It is thus obvious, the transformation to happen in the world requires more than just going to Church.

A church leader's success and greatness are not measured by how well he or she can preach or teach, or the number of members attached to the vision. Greatness is a result of servitude. We as Ministers of the gospel have to go beyond our need to feel good about how we preach. This is a drug and many of us become addicted to it. It is not about us – we are assigned to lead people out of the wilderness. It is very easy to fall in love with your own voice. Our role and function are no different from Moses and Aaron, Joshua and Caleb. Moses taught the people to understand the mind and heart of God. He did not teach or preach to make himself feel good or to be invited. His heart's cry was to see the people delivered from their issues and to be deeply cleansed from the effects of their issues, so that they could enter the Promised Land. Our success is measured by how many people under our leadership are coming out of the wilderness to enter a kingdom of God reality on the earth.

My encouragement to anyone who is reading this book is to get the film of Moses leading the Israelites out of Egypt. Watching this film will help you to relate to the Church appropriately. God is not responsible for how long we stay in the wilderness. We determine how long we stay in the wilderness dimension, just like a university student determines how long it would take him or her to obtain their degree. This person needs to connect with some of their weaknesses, limitations, hindrances, obstacles, challenges, problems, trials and hardship that need to be overcome, that is, things that can possibly sabotage his or her ability to meet all the requirements and expectations to graduate from the university and progress in life. We need to confront our issues head-on to become free, as issues will run our lives if we deny them. We also need to give attention to our negative relationships, as it generates negative energies which slow down and limit our progression in life. This journey is the long walk to freedom. I am a firm believer that **"why"** is more powerful than **"how"**. Many people know what to do, yet they are not doing it, simply because they lack a strong enough why. Why deals with the purpose and how deals with a method. Teaching methods are spoon feeding, teaching life giving principles are empowerment. Application flows out of a deep understanding. It is purpose that provides passion, power, drive and meaning to life, with power being the ability to make things happen. Why am I saying all of this? I say this because I sense a restrain not to talk about how we led our people out of the wilderness; instead, I feel the freedom to provide some outcomes, so that you can begin with the end in mind. This is exactly how God treats us: He showed the Israelites a glimpse of the Promised Land, but He did not tell them how to get there. He gave them forward thinking and rewind them back. This is what predestination is all about. He has chosen us before the foundation of the earth and allowed us to live apart from Him, before He saved us.

SEEK TO DEVELOP HUMAN RESOURCES

This is the wisdom that I have gained from the children of this world when I was working for one of the world's top motor manufacturing companies. They first build a few cars to establish their quality standards before they go for mass production. If they would go for mass production first they will suffer loss, because of poor quality standards. Quality should precede quantity, it is plain common sense. We build quantity with our hands, but quality is something that proceeds from the heart. It is an attitude. This same principle can be applied to building a ministry. The focus should be on quality first before we should go for quantity. In this way, we can create a "monkey-see, monkey-do" environment, which make it easy to uphold high quality standards with less effort. People do what they see, simply because we impart who we are, not what we say. I have applied this wisdom by not having an evangelistic focus, and I only worked with the people that God was sending into our ministry. I was willing to have a small ministry for a very long time, instead of having too many people to work with. We are now ready to receive the masses, because we have enough quality people that can model our culture and ministry quality standards. I have personally witnessed big ministries that have no real influence over their people's attitudinal issues, and not being able to deal with members' personal problems that cast a bad reflection on the ministry. Our ministry success is measured by how well our people behave themselves, not by how many people we have.

My working experiences were a life school that was getting me ready for ministry. I was then able to train, develop, equip and empower our people to be there for others and to work effectively and efficiently with the issues of incoming new members. I poured my whole life into the development of twelve leaders for many years, of which I form part, and had no ambition for a big ministry. My greatest drive was to see people being changed and transformed by the power that God has given me. We are now growing a big ministry with no attachment to numbers, because our strongest drive is to see people free. We do not advertise our ministry, because our vision is not tarrying anymore, it is speaking loudly to all the inhabitants of our land. I am not sure that I know anything more powerful than to see failures become successful, poor and broke people becoming prosperous, dependent people becoming independent, independent people become interdependent, weak people becoming strong and well able. This has been the outcome of the work our people did in the lives of many others. A leader's ultimate goal is to get things done through others. There is a TV programme called "Starting Over" that is being done by a team of life coaches. This can be a helpful tool to Church leaders to see how we should work with people that are totally messed up and are unable to make a success of their lives. I am getting deeply touched whenever I watch this programme, because it reminds me of our many years in the wilderness.

WE NEED TO DEVELOP AND EQUIP PEOPLE

THAT...

- can mentor others.
- can father and mother others.
- are wired to disciple others accurately.
- can assist and support people to set up their own businesses.
- can be life coaches.
- can teach ABET (unschooled).
- has a strong mercy gift to support and empower single parent mothers.
- has a strong mercy gift and a heart for street children.
- has a strong mercy gift and a heart for the poor.
- can teach life skills.
- can provide wise counsel to others (not the type of counseling that creates dependence on others).
- can help people to discover themselves.
- can assist people to make transitions.
- can teach and show our people how to work with money.
- can teach people how to convert their salary income into portfolio and passive income.
- can teach and show people how to raise up their kids.
- can teach and show our people how to have a good marriage.
- can assist people to deal effectively with their unfinished business and unresolved emotional issues.
- are called to be apostles, prophets, evangelist, pastors and teachers.
- can teach people how to convert their life liabilities into assets.

The wilderness is meant to make us become sons of God (accurate representations of God) who can shine as lights in a crooked and perverse generation and to make us ready to do kingdom business to occupy all influential places in the world, until Christ comes back to receive the Kingdom to deliver it up to God, even the Father. **Then**

cometh the end, when he shall have delivered up the kingdom to God, even the Father; when he shall have put down all rule and all authority and power (1Corinthians 15:24).

SKILLS BELIEVERS NEED TO HELP THEM TO GET OUT OF THE WILDERNESS

Skill is the ability to do something well, and it gets developed under pressure and through consistency. Consistency is the mother of skill. Every circumstance and any unfavorable situation are meant to provide us a schooling opportunity. Believe me, life becomes so much more excited when we start to think in this manner. You are a king and a priest unto God; therefore anything that happens to you comes to serve you.

Here are some vital life skills to help you make a transition from the wilderness into a kingdom of God reality on earth:

- Stop taking yourself too serious and don't make anything become too personal.
- Learn to be lightly attached to material things.
- Learn to deal with conflict constructively by learning conflict handling skills.
- Develop emotional intelligence and be real with yourself regarding your emotions.
- Be proactive in all your dealings.
- Learn to deal quickly with offences.
- Learn to forgive very quickly and move on.
- Learn how to die successfully to self.
- Learn how to walk effectively through trials, tribulation or any hardship.
- Be responsible and never blame and accuse anyone for what is happening to you, irrespective of who is wrong.

- Learn to be transparent – do not walk around with issues for longer than one day.
- Accept total responsibility for all your shortcomings, weaknesses and negative past life experiences. We can only change what we accept.
- Become a relational person.
- Constantly change your thinking to align it with the Word of God and life giving principles.

BELIEVERS ARE READY TO COME OUT OF THE WILDERNESS IF THE FOLLOWING THINGS ARE ESTABLISHED IN THEIR LIVES:

The Bible says this about Caleb and Joshua, who made a transition from the wilderness into the Promised Land: They had a different spirit. **But my servant Caleb, because he had a different spirit in him, and has been true to me with all his heart, him I will take into that land into which he went, and his seed will have it for their heritage** (Numbers 14: 24). The following list represents a different spirit (attitude) to make a transition into the Promised Land:

- zero rebellion.
- well able to respect and follow leadership and clearly defined instruction.
- minds have been renewed and have an ability to tap into the mind of Christ.
- not to walk by sight.
- such people know their life calling and themselves.
- They know their temperament make-up and how to side step their weaknesses and to maximize their strengths.

- They have a very healthy self-esteem, self-image and a sense of personal honor – without these things a person will never be able to stand on their own.
- They are sons of God with visible evidence that they are being led by the Spirit. **For as many as are led by the Spirit of God, they are the sons of God** (Romans 8:14).
- They do not have a need for approval and to be affirmed by others all the time. Affirmations from others are mere confirmations.
- They are able to relate to whosoever – have strong people skills.
- They enjoy reading, studying and meditating on the Word of God daily as a lifestyle.
- They have an established prayer life.
- They know the voice of God.
- They have discovered their anointing and their place of grace.
- Know how to manage their thought and emotional life.
- Have been discipled and can disciple others effectively.
- Can deal constructively with any kind of conflict.
- Forgive easily and do not hold any grudges and offences.
- Does not get easily hurt and offended.
- They walk their talk.
- They have a growth plan that they follow and are able to assist others to develop a growth plan for themselves.
- They are free from blaming and accusing others for their life situations – they are able to take personal responsibility for any situation they find themselves in. They know it is not about who is right, but what is right.
- They think win-win and are proactive and assertive in their dealings with people and situations.
- They completed the sanctification process thoroughly – mental cleansing, emotional cleansing, attitudinal cleansing, character and core cleansing.
- They show clear signs of the fruit of the Spirit in their lives.

- Work cooperatively in teams and has the ability to lead a team.
- Has a clearly defined purpose, vision and mission statement.
- Have clearly defined life and financial goals.
- Have an established set of core values and priorities
- Have an ability to meet all eight areas of their basic human needs – spiritual, mental, emotional, family (spouse and children), finances, vocational, physical (health and fitness) and social needs.
- They know how to work with their finances and would rather sow for what they need or want instead of buying on credit.
- They are established in all basic life skills – communication, conflict handling, relational, people skills, good reading habit, financial, leadership, management, team work, time management, ministerial, gifts of the Spirit, etc.
- They are fully equipped by the five fold ministry to do the work of the ministry to edify the Body of Christ.
- Their lives are well structured and have a filing system concerning all things that pertain to their lives.
- They live fruitful lives, which is the starting place of our kingdom assignments.
- They are Kingdom minded.

This has been our focus over the many years in the Wilderness. I have always wondered why I have so much work to do and how some leaders get it right to have so little to do. Making disciples is no easy task, yet it is most fulfilling. Getting more members has become the most important focus to many of us. It is possible to be saved and delivered and still live a very unfulfilling life, simply because discipline is the key to a successful, happy and fulfilled life. Jesus knows why it is so important to make disciples. This assignment is called the great commission, not the great suggestion. Without making disciples, all our people will die in the Wilderness and never come to enjoy the good life. **And Jesus came and spake unto them, saying, All power is given unto me in heaven and in**

earth. Go ye therefore, and teach all nations, baptizing them in the name of the Father, and of the Son, and of the Holy Ghost: Teaching them to observe all things whatsoever I have commanded you: and, lo, I am with you always, even unto the end of the world. Amen (Matthew 28:18-20). Let us honor our Lord Jesus by doing what He has called us to do. **Ye are my friends, if ye do whatsoever I command you** (John 15:14). It is an honor and privilege to be a friend of Jesus Christ our Lord.

I would like to tell a short real life story that I have read about, which was told by a woman who works with the deep issues and scars that are affecting people's lives very negatively. This story really touched me very deeply, and it makes me to realise anew and afresh as to how important it is to disciple believers. There are just some things that Jesus is not going to do for people, simply because He assigned us to do it for Him by making disciples. Doubtless to say that He does reach out to some whom He then assigns to reach out to many others. Joyce Meyer comes to mind of those who have been assigned to teach hurting people. There are many, many believers that are going nowhere in life, and they are still carrying deep wounds for many years without getting healed, simply because no one is reaching out to them. I trust that this story would make you connect with the great importance of discipleship, as discipleship provides a closed circle where people feel free to open up their lives because they have learnt to trust the discipler.

Let's call this young lad Frankie. His family was extremely poor and unable to provide the family with the basics, including food. At the age of eight, he got a job at a local shop, helping with small tasks. His family was deeply grateful for the extra ten dollars a week and this made him feel real proud of himself. However, it so happened that the owner of the shop began to make sexual advances toward Frankie. He knew what the owner was doing to him was not right, yet his family was now counting on his weekly contributions to the household. He finally found the courage to describe to his mother what he had to do in order to earn his weekly contributions. His mother responded by forbidding him ever to speak of such things again. The family members were counting on him keeping that job she said. Frankie remained at the shop until he was thirteen years old. Can you feel the pain?

The effects of his abuse extended into his student life. He barely made it through his years in high school, and at fifteen he was a dropout. Alcohol helped repress Frankie's nightmare experiences of being sexually molested and calmed his nerves. As a coping mechanism, he turned to alcohol. This is the enemy's solution to humanities' suffering and pain. Getting saved delivers people from alcohol, but it does not take away the pain and the wounds, unless someone cares enough to walk with such a person or, unless the Lord step in, which are not always the case. Frankie is but just a mere sample size of a population of people that walks around with such deep pain and suffering, and there are many of them in the Church. The way out for Frankie is to find someone to confide in and to find a sense of security and the freedom to open up and allow that dark chapter of his life to be poured out of him. Shame and indescribable pain prevent many from opening up the dark chapters of their lives. The solution is people who are skilled in working with such cases and who are able to give the gift of confidentiality.

BECOMING ESTABLISHED ON A FIRM FOUNDATION:

I hereby would like to encourage you my friend to make the most of your Wilderness seasons with the knowing that the Lord will bring you out in due season. Peter revealed to us a process that would bring us to a place where we would be firmly fixed on a foundation that will not be moved by winds or floods. Let's read what Peter is saying to us:

1Peter 5:10 But the God of all grace, who hath called us unto his eternal glory by Christ Jesus, after that ye have suffered a while, make you perfect, establish, strengthen, settle *you*.

1. **Suffering** (the intensity of the wilderness experience)
2. **Make you perfect** - trials, tribulation, hardship, affliction, etc. are God's tools to make us perfect. It is the devil that separates us from God – God uses the same devil to bring us closer to Him through his weapons, trials, tribulations, etc. (Read Isaiah 54: 17)
3. **Establish you** – to render immovable
4. **Strengthen you** – give you strength to bear and handle any situation.
5. **Settle you** – to be firmly fixed on a foundation that will not be moved by winds or floods.

These are five stages we travel to become established in any area of our lives where we are currently suffering. The numerical meaning of five stands for grace, which is **God's** riches at **Christ's** expense. This is the grace that would bring you into ruling and reigning in the place where you have suffered, and you will be able to minister to those who are also suffering. Our misery becomes our ministry. **For if by one man's offence death reigned by one; much more they which receive abundance of grace and of the gift of righteousness shall reign in life by one, Jesus Christ** (Romans 5:17).

Chapter 5

YOU ARE THE CHURCH

What? Know you not that your body is the temple of the Holy Ghost which is in you, which ye have of God, and ye are not your own? (1Cor 6:19).

I previously mentioned that church literally means "those called out," and often means an assembly or congregation. However, our focus in this chapter is going to be on the individual person as the Church. The Church is not a building where the "called out" gather to worship. **Howbeit the Most High dwells not in temples made with hands; as saith the prophet** (Acts 7:48). Hereby know we that we dwell in Him, and He in us, because He has given us of His Spirit. His manifested presence in our gathering in temples made with hands manifest because of this treasure in earthen vessels. We are a dwelling place of God or a habitation of God through the Spirit.

We are three-dimensional - spirit, soul and body, with the soul representing the second dimension, which is the Church or the Wilderness. The holy place in the tabernacle also represents the second dimension. It is in this dimension that the Lord makes us become holy by and through the Holy Spirit. We are called to be a chosen race, a royal priesthood, **a holy nation**, peculiar people for God's own possession, that we may proclaim the excellence of Him who called us out of darkness into His marvellous light. Therefore the soul needs to be cleansed for our lights to shine. With the pure He will show Himself pure. **And He shall sit *as* a refiner and purifier of silver: and he shall purify the sons of Levi, and purge them as gold and silver, that they may offer unto the LORD an offering in righteousness** (Mal 3:3). Jesus washed us in His own blood and made us kings and priests, which is to say that we too have obtained the role of the sons of Levi (Rev 1: 6). We too have to go through a process of refining. It is this dimension of our being that can cause us to become stuck in the Wilderness dimension if we refuse to be cleansed by the Lord. The Lord our God is a consuming fire.

This cleansing process is also called sanctification, which is a two-fold process. This two-fold process speaks about a subjective and an objective sanctification experience. You cannot make yourself holy, neither will God purge you. This simply means that, there is a process under which we have to subject ourselves to the working of the Holy Spirit to make us holy. Jesus also said that the Word that I speak to you is Spirit and have already cleansed you. Secondly, we have to purge ourselves from issues that has defiled and contaminated us through negative life experiences. The Holy Spirit and the Holy Scripture's cleansing are a subjective cleansing or sanctification, whilst purging is an objective sanctification process. A spiritual subjective experience happens independently from our abilities. An objective experience requires individual effort. A spiritual breakthrough is simply the coming together of a subjective and an objective experience. Spirit plus natural equals the supernatural. This means that we need both the spirit and the natural. Jesus is not ashamed to call us brethren once we have been sanctified by Him. **For both He that sanctifies and they who are sanctified are all of one: for which cause He is not ashamed to call them brethren** (Heb 2:11). Is Jesus ashamed of those who have not been sanctified? The Book of Proverbs answers this question: **A wise son maketh a glad father: but a foolish son *is* the heaviness (sorrow; to bring grief; is an affliction; to make sad) of his mother** (Proverbs 10: 11). This means a person who is unsanctified brings grief or sorrow to the One, who sanctifies. An unsanctified person is one who still has a lot of undealt issues in his or her life. This includes issues pertaining to unforgiveness, offences, anger, bitterness, jealousy, envy, and such like.

THE WORD OF GOD SANCTIFIES US:

- And for their sakes I sanctify myself, that they also might be sanctified through the truth (John 17:19).
- For it is sanctified by the word of God and prayer (1Tim 4:5).
- Now ye are clean through the word which I have spoken unto you (John 15:3/Eph 5: 26).

THE HOLY SPIRIT SANCTIFIES US, AND WE SHOULD PURGE OURSELVES:

- That I should be the minister of Jesus Christ to the Gentiles, ministering to the gospel of God, that the offering up of the Gentiles might be acceptable, being sanctified by the Holy Ghost (Rom 15:16).
- If a man, therefore, purges himself from these, he shall be a vessel unto honour, sanctified, and meet for the master's use, *and* prepared unto every good work (2Timothy 2:21).

YOUR SOUL IS THE STARTING PLACE OF EVERYTHING

We read in 3John 1 that we prosper or succeed in life in direct proportion to the condition of our soul. In other words, soul prosperity leads to outer prosperity, whilst contrary, soul poverty leads to outer poverty, and so forth. Our bodies are a mere junction between the invisible and the visible. It is either members of unrighteousness or righteousness. We dare not take soul issues lightly - our thoughts will create our attitude, and our attitude leads to action that is either good or bad. Therefore our attitudes and thoughts must all be constantly changing for the better as we aim to measure up with God's plan for us.

OUR SOUL CONSISTS OF OUR MIND, WILL AND EMOTIONS

Mind:

The mind consists of a conscious and a subconscious mind. The subconscious mind is the heart of the mind or the spirit of the mind. This is where the renewing of the mind needs to take place to become a new and different person with a fresh newness in all we do and think. **And be renewed in the spirit of your mind** (Eph 4:23). And be not conformed to this world: but be ye transformed by the renewing of your mind, that ye may prove what *is* that good, and acceptable, and perfect, will of God - Romans 12:2. The Word of God is pure. Therefore, it purifies the mind and heart. **Thy word is very pure** (Psalm 119:140a). Jesus said, now you are clean through the Word which I have spoken unto you (John 15:3).

Emotions:

Our thoughts are highly energetic; it creates emotions, which are energy in motion that influences our attitudes and ultimately our action. Emotional intelligence enables a person to assess his or her feelings in a positive light, which result in the feelings not becoming distorted. Negative feelings reveal to us that we are thinking negatively about something. Positive feelings reveal to us that our thinking is positive. As such, we should learn to think what we think.

Will:

Our will is our decision making faculty, which is being influenced by our thinking and how we feel in any given situation. We should therefore develop the disciplines to cast our negative emotions upon the Lord and to consult God in our decision making and also check what the Word of God has to say about the decisions we make. We should also seek the counsel of mature believers to help us align our will with the divine will. You are a powerful human being when your will and the divine will are one.

THE GOAL OF SANCTIFICATION:

The ultimate goal of this intense emotional process is to get to a place that there is nothing of the devil in you. This sucker was very strategic about your life. He has planted some seeds in your life to be able to press your buttons anytime he wishes to mess you up. These seeds must be uprooted, taken out and thrown out of our lives. It works exactly like the TV and the remote control. The TV has a sensor in it that gives the remote control power over the TV to switch it over to any channel, or to pause or stop the TV. The remote control has no power over the TV if you remove the sensor. In the same way the devil has no control over us if we remove the seeds he has planted in us. The devil could not control Jesus, because Jesus had nothing of the devil within Him. This is exactly what Jesus said in John 14: 30 - **Hereafter, I will not talk much with you: for the prince of this world comes, and hath nothing in me.** So this is what Jesus actually said: There is in me no principle or feeling that accords with his, and nothing therefore by which he can prevail. Temptation has only power because there are some principles in us which accord with the designs of the tempter, and which may be excited by presenting corresponding objects until our virtue be overcome. Where there is no such propensity, temptation has no power. As the principles of Jesus were wholly on the side of virtue, the meaning here may be that, though he had the natural appetites of man, his virtue was so supreme that Satan "had nothing in him" which could constitute any danger that he would be led into sin, and that there was no fear of the result of the conflict before him. This is a good place to be and God has prepared a process for us to get to such a place. That process is called sanctification, cleansing or holiness.

WE ARE NEW TESTAMENT PRIESTS UNTO GOD

The priest in the Old Testament served in the Holy Place and in this place were three furniture pieces. There was a seven lamp-stand, table of show bread and table of incense. These furniture pieces were natural things which had spiritual significance. They are now unseen spiritual realities in our day and time. We are now the temple of God; therefore, these furniture pieces dwell within us, because Jesus Christ, Who is in us, is the true tabernacle of God (Col 1: 27).

THE SEVEN LAMP STANDS REPRESENTS THE HOLY SPIRIT.

- The Holy Spirit lives in us. What? Know you not that your body is the temple of the Holy Ghost which is in you, which ye have of God, and ye are not your own? (1Co 6:19)
- The seven lamp stands also represents the seven spirits of God, which is at work in us. They are seven independent manifestations of the Spirit. Isaiah the prophet prophecy about these seven Spirits that would be on Jesus, which are now in us. See Isaiah 11: 1-4
    1. The Spirit of the Lord
    2. The Spirit of wisdom
    3. The Spirit of understanding
    4. The Spirit of counsel
    5. The Spirit of might.
    6. The Spirit of knowledge
    7. The Spirit of the fear of the Lord.

THE TABLE OF SHOW BREAD REPRESENTS THE WORD OF GOD.

- Our hearts are now the fleshly table on which God has written His words with the Spirit. "Forasmuch as ye are manifestly declared to be the epistle of Christ ministered by us, written not with ink, but with the Spirit of the living God; not in tables of stone, but in fleshy tables of the heart" - 2Cor 3:3.

THE TABLE OF INCENSE REPRESENTS THE PRAYERS OF THE SAINTS.

- John talked about the One who would come and baptize us with fire. This is the fire that burns the incense of our prayers. And another angel came and stood at the altar, having a golden censer; and there was given unto him much incense, that he should offer *it* with the prayers of all saints upon the golden altar which was before the throne. And the smoke of the incense, *which came* with the prayers of the saints, ascended up before God out of the angel's hand - Rev 8:3-4

We are being cleansed and sanctified whenever we fellowship with the Holy Spirit that is within us and when we read, study and meditate on the Word of God and through our daily prayer life as we release incense that ascends up to God. The Apostle Paul encourages and exhorts us to seek those things which are above, where Christ sits on the right hand of God, and that we should always set our affection on things above, not on things on the earth. Those things that are above are the things of the tabernacle that God showed Moses when He instructed him to build Him a tabernacle so that He could dwell among His people. We allow God to dwell among us through our Spirit life, Word life and prayer life, because these are the things that are above. We must set our affection on these things. The things on earth are the things that the Gentiles seek for. Therefore, we should take no thought about what we shall eat? Or, what we shall drink? Or, wherewithal we shall be clothed? For after all these things do the Gentiles seek: Our heavenly Father knows that we have need of all these things. There is life in the Spirit, life in the Word and life in having an establish prayer life. Let's set our affection on these things. Let heaven fill your thoughts; don't spend your time worrying about things down here. Don't lower yourself to a Pagan level. We are being built together for a dwelling place of God through the Spirit whenever we set our affections on things above. We grow when we get our nourishment and strength from God.

THE HEART IS DECEITFUL ABOVE ALL THINGS

The Proverb writer tells us to guard our heart above ALL things, because out of it spring or jump the issues of life (Proverbs 4: 23). The issues in our hearts are our future circumstances. I consider it a life skill to guard your heart. I have learnt and developed this life skill, but yet some things just slips in unnoticed, and I am always greatly surprised when these issues shows up in my life. This makes me to understand why Jeremiah said the following words: **The heart is deceitful above all things, and desperately wicked: who can know it? Jeremiah 17:9.** Desperately wicked means morally sick. A man's heart is a mystery – God alone can fathom it. It is always a painful thing when He shows us what is in our hearts. It is best to purge yourself as quick as possible once you become aware of the things that can defile and contaminate your heart. Your heart is your greatest asset: guard it above all things. That's why it is so important for us to walk in the fear (reverential respect) of the Lord, which is the beginning of wisdom. The Book of Acts contains four spiritual pillars that would bring the fear of God (reverential respect and honor) upon our soul. It reads like this: **And they continued steadfastly in the apostles' doctrine and fellowship, and in breaking of bread, and in prayers. 43 And fear came upon every soul: and many wonders and signs were done by the apostles. 44 And all that believed were together, and had all things common - Acts 2:42-44**

THE FOUR SPIRITUAL PILLARS:

1. Continue steadfastly in the apostle's doctrine
2. And in fellowship
3. And in breaking of bread
4. And in prayer.

What is the apostle's doctrine? The answer to this question is found in Acts 5: 42, which tells us what the apostles were teaching when they were meeting in the temple and in every house. **And daily in the temple, and in every house, they ceased not to teach and preach Jesus Christ - Acts 5:42.** They taught and preached Jesus Christ, which are two dimensions about Jesus. Jesus is an outer court dimension and Christ is a holy place dimension. Teaching educates the mind and preaching educates the heart. Scripture tells that we should love the Lord with all our mind and heart; therefore, ministers of God should always do both teaching and preaching to ensure balance. I have observed that people who only preached are very zealous, but they lack wisdom in their day to day life. Their minds have not been properly shaped because they do not get instructed by a teacher. Jesus taught, preached and healed – we can see this throughout the four Gospels.

THE FIVE CLEANSING LEVELS:

1. Mental cleansing
2. Attitudinal cleansing
3. Emotional cleansing
4. Character cleansing
5. Core cleansing.

Let's look in the Bible for an example of a person who had a mental and attitudinal problem and how negatively it has affected his life. The things we think create our attitude, as we bring about what we think about. It might be shocking to say that this person is called John the Baptist, because this is what Jesus said about this man: Verily, I say unto you, Among them that are born of women there hath not risen a greater than John the Baptist: notwithstanding he that is least in the kingdom of heaven is greater than he – (Mat 11:11). And this is what John said about Jesus: The next day John saw Jesus coming unto him, and saith, Behold the Lamb of God, which takes away the sin of the world (John 1:29). John beheld the greatness of Jesus and said that he was not worthy to bear Jesus' shoes. **I indeed baptize you with water unto repentance: but he that cometh after me is mightier than I, whose shoes, I am not worthy to bear: he shall baptize you with the Holy Ghost, and with fire - Matthew 3:11:**

It first sounds very confusing to me that Jesus said that there has not risen a greater than John, but yet He says that the least in the kingdom of God is greater than John. Well, the lights switched on for me, and I made a connection that even the least in the kingdom of God are kings and priests unto God. John was a great prophet, but this great prophet could not enter the kingdom of God, because he had mental and attitudinal problems which he did not resolve. John was put in prison by Herod. Let's read it: **For Herod had laid hold on John, and bound him, and put *him* in prison for Herodias' sake, his brother Philip's wife - Mat 14:3.** John being in prison was a divine set up for John to see what was in his heart, because the worst of us are being revealed under severe pressure. Fire exposes snakes. This situation was John's opportunity to purge himself from wrong thinking and his negative attitude. It is John who saw Jesus and said, "Behold the Lamb of God, which takes away the sin of the world." It is also John who said these words when he was under severe pressure: **Now when John had heard in the prison the works of Christ, he sent two of his disciples, And said unto him, Art thou he that should come, or do we look for another? - Mat**

11:2-3. It is written: Blessed is he, whosoever shall not be offended in Jesus (Mat 11:6).

Now let's look at how Jesus responded to John's disciples' question and see how Jesus was affected by the news that John was beheaded. **Jesus answered and said unto them, Go and show John again those things which ye do hear and see: The blind receive their sight, and the lame walk, the lepers are cleansed, and the deaf hear, the dead are raised up, and the poor have the gospel preached to them - Mat 11:4-5.** Jesus was deeply hurt by the news that John was beheaded, because He departed by ship into a desert place apart to console (Matt 14: 12-13). It is a critical thing to walk around in this world with mental and attitudinal issues, because such things bring great destruction on us. These things feed our ego mind, and it is not good for a man to be led by his ego mind, which is our lower carnal nature.

Can you imagine how our corporate gatherings would be if each believer would diligently take care of his or her inner temple (soul-dimension) and allow God to be God in us? The mystery of godliness is God manifest in the flesh – He is a treasure in an earthen vessel, and He wants to manifest Himself in this world through us. In order that at the moment, by the Church, the angelic rulers and powers in the heavenly world might learn of His wisdom in all its different forms through us. We have all mistakenly misplaced our focus on an outer building and have neglected the temple within. Chapter 10 will focus on the corporate body of believers – the Congregation of the Lord. **However, now, by the physical death of his Son, God has made you His friends, in order to bring you, holy, pure, and faultless, into his presence (Col 1:22).** It is important that we should work with God to make us holy, pure, and faultless. God longs to have sons in this world that are blameless and harmless, who might shine as lights in a crooked and perverse generation for His name sake.

Chapter 6

WE ARE LIVING IN THREE WORLDS.

We live in three worlds at the same time. These are: **our outer world** (physical world) **our inner world** (kingdom within); **our spiritual world** (heavenly places). The word of God tells us that we are seated in heavenly places in Christ Jesus. **And hath raised us up together, and made us sit together in heavenly places in Christ Jesus** (Ephesians 2: 6). Are we all deeply aware that we have been raised to such a high exalted place? This reality is far beyond human understanding; therefore, the mind will only begin to conceive it through much meditation, contemplation and consistent confession.

We are three-dimensional beings, just like our Creator – Father, Son and Holy Spirit. We are body, soul and spirit. Our physical body gives us access and connection to the physical world; our soul dimension represents our deep inner world; our spirit gives us access and divine connection into the heavenly places in Christ. God created man to have dominion over the physical world, but if we do not understand how to exercise dominion within the inner world (kingdom within), we will not be successful in exercising dominion over our outer world. **Like a city broken into and left without a**

wall, so is a person who lacks self-control – Proverbs 25: 28.

Furthermore, take note, that as well as we are living in three worlds at the same time we also, in a true sense, live three lives at the same time.

- **Our deep inner life** - this is where we connect with ourselves, what we are thinking, feeling, imagining, experiencing deep within us and our deep inner beliefs. Our self-image, self-worth, self-esteem, and self-respect, which can either, be an empowered or disempowered sense of self and our sense of right and wrong (conscience). In other words, our inner guidance – intuitive senses and our sensitivity to the Holy Spirit.
- **Our private life** – or personal life which may be lived alone, or with our spouse, family or close friends.
- **Our public life**, where we interact with people at our workplace or market place, at church, in our community and at social events.

Our most significant life is our deep inner life, with victory in this life preceding private victory, and private victory preceding public victory. Authenticity is when we truly live these three lives in total harmony. This means that I sincerely express myself to my family members in accordance with who I truly am within, and the person I am in my public life is exactly who I am at home.

Not understanding these three worlds can cause much difficulty in living our lives effectively. **Understanding is the key to effective living.** The book of Proverbs talks a lot about the importance of understanding. Proverbs 4: 7c says, **...and in all your getting, get understanding.** We all have many things we want in life, but to understand should be our priority. In reality, life, and the getting of other things, becomes much easier when we have understanding.

We can have all the wealth in the world, but **...to get understanding is to be chosen rather than silver –** Proverbs 16: 16 , because if we lack understanding about our life's circumstances, we will be miserable irrespective of riches. A few verses further on, understanding is likened to a wellspring of life to anyone who has it. Therefore, true understanding creates real life.

The best thing that can happen to us in times of trouble is to have peace; **...a man** (person) **of understanding holds his peace** (Proverbs 11: 12), and in doing so, we will be able to think ourselves out of any situation. The Bible calls this kind of peace **...God's peace, which exceeds anything we can understand** (Philippians 4: 7). In other words, the human mind cannot comprehend this kind of peace, because we normally lack peace when we are in trouble, but a person of understanding will have peace and will accordingly be able to draw counsel from his heart. This peace also refers to keeping quiet or shutting our lips, ensuring we stay blameless in a situation. As Proverbs 10:19 states; **Where there is much talk, there will be no end to sin, but he who keeps his mouth shut does wisely.**

The importance of having a full understanding concerning the **outer**, the **inner** and the **spiritual** worlds cannot be overestimated, and the consequences of any lack of awareness and understanding will result in us being unconsciously controlled by these worlds. As everything in life is always 'managed', the question is: Who is managing? If we are not managing, we will **be** managed. Management is either internal or external. As an example; crime is the result of people who do not exercise internal management. Therefore, the police force must step in to provide external management or government.

The most effective way to carry out our dominion mandate is to study these three worlds to gain understanding so we can relate properly to each of them. Application will then naturally flow out of that understanding. Just as there will be conflict in any relationship if individuals can't relate properly to each other, there will also be constant conflict in our lives if we cannot relate properly to our three worlds.

In reality, we can only **see** one of these three worlds, which is the outer world. We experience our inner world by what we **feel** and the spiritual world by what we **sense or discern,** if we have developed the ability to discern what is happening around us. The outer world gives us feedback from both our inner world and the spiritual world. Those who do not understand this relationship, will try to fix what they see in their outer world, not realizing their problem stems from one or both other worlds.

It is like a person who goes into a room full of spider-webs and decides to clean it up. However, when he returns in three days he is aghast to see it full of webs again! Unless he finds the spider, he will have to consistently return to clean the room! This is going to get very tiring! The old adage of "where there is a root, there will always be fruit", is common sense that dictates that we should find the root cause to **permanently** eliminate the problem. Kill the spider!

Instead of trying to fix our outer world, we should be fixing ourselves (our inner world), and get connected with the spiritual world through prayer. We should work harder on ourselves than anything else. Whatever we experience in our outer world is a consequence of what we experience in our inner world and the spiritual world. If we can identify the problem within and fix it, the outer world will re-adjust itself accordingly.

Here is a practical day to day example to illustrate this:

The condition of your cupboard or garage where you pack your personal things is your immediate outer world, mirroring your inner world. In fact, this 'outer' place is your first level of feedback regarding your inner world. If your immediate outer world looks disorderly it shows that your emotional world is perhaps in disorder also. Your cupboard or garage will therefore remain in this condition until you bring order to your emotional world. The day this happens you will experience some real inner drive to also bring order to your cupboard or garage or car. Have you ever noticed that whenever you feel good about yourself, you have an inner drive to clean everything around you? The drive to clean up is a result of you taking care of your inner world.

The reality is, the outer world aligns itself to what happens within us. Whatever is real on the inside will become a reality on the outside. It is also interesting to note how long our cupboard or garage stays neat and orderly after clearing it. This feedback can help us assess ourselves in terms of our emotional stability. If it only lasts for a few days or a day, it may tell us we are again emotionally unstable. However, if we are able to maintain order for some time, perhaps it shows a measure of emotional stability.

WHAT HAPPENS WITHIN US LINKS US TO THE OTHER TWO WORLDS

- Whatever we feel as real on the inside will become a reality in our outer world.
- Whatever we feel as real on the inside will also attract things in the outer world of the same nature as that which we feel within. Example: if I feel rejected, I will attract rejected people to myself who will eventually reject me, because people impart what they feel within.
- Whatever we feel as real on the inside makes us open to attract things in the spiritual world related to what we feel within. This can be positive as well as negative.

The principles we need to understand about these links are: we have no control over what happens **to** us, but we have control over what happens **within** us. This brings us back to the fact that everything starts within us. Have you noticed how many things changed in your life when you accepted Jesus to come live in you? As within, so it will be without.

IDENTIFY IN WHICH GROUP YOU FALL:

The first group of people is totally unaware of these three worlds. They think things just happen to them because it is just the way life is. This is a wrong belief, because nothing just happens, we make things happen consciously or unconsciously.

The second group of people is aware of only two worlds; what happens in them and what happens around them (outer world). These people are totally unaware of the spiritual world. In fact, living life inside-out can produce a level of success, but being connected with the third world (spiritual world) will produce far greater success.

The third group of people is fully aware of the spiritual world as well as the outer world, but they are unaware of their inner world. People who fall into this group normally blame the devil and other people for what happens to them. What really happens when we play the blame and accuse game? We give our personal power away to the things we blame or accuse, but if we take full responsibility for what happens to us, irrespective of who is right or wrong, we actually use our personal power to make right, what is wrong. This is good advice to the third group of people. Personal power gives us access into spiritual power, because God will not entrust anyone with spiritual power (anointing) if they cannot be trusted with personal power (responsibility). This is where corruption normally comes in with government officials who have not shown themselves faithful with personal power, therefore they can't really handle all the external power that comes with their position.

The fourth group of people is fully aware of their inner world, outer world and the spiritual world. People in this group who have mastered their understanding of all three worlds will be the ones who will truly rule and reign in life and on the earth. Having dominion is the destiny of the human race. Our goal should be to be in a proper relationship with the three worlds that we are living in, all at the same time, thus learning how to balance our lives.

Whatever group you find yourself, please make sure to make a transition into the fourth group of people by giving careful attention to all three worlds.

Chapter 7

GOD IS DYNAMIC, NOT STATIC

*And the LORD went before them by day
in a pillar of a cloud, to lead them the way;
and by night in a pillar of fire, to give
them light; to go by day and night:
Exodus 13:21*

Again we can in fact see that God's dealings with the Israelites show us a natural picture of what is happening spiritually to us. God was forever moving His people from one level to another level in the wilderness dimension, just as by day in a pillar of cloud and by night in a pillar of fire. God did not change in this regard; He remains the same yesterday, today and forever (Heb 13: 8). God is still in the business of moving His people from glory to glory, just as by the Spirit of the Lord. We get stuck in life when we do not move on with what God is doing in the earth through His people. We called it a move of God in our day and times. Every single move of God is intended to move His Church out of the Wilderness dimension into Her Promised Land, which is the Kingdom of God. A movement means the act of changing location from one place to another. The only permanent things in life are CHANGE. **However, the saints of the most High shall take the kingdom, and possess**

the kingdom for ever, even for ever and ever - Daniel 7:18.
This kingdom will not pass away like the other kingdoms.

The moves of God were never ever intended to become a denomination to dominate the people of God and to keep them in one place year after year and to separate them from the rest of the Body of Christ. This word "denomination" means a religious congregation having its own organization and a distinctive faith, or distinguished from others. Distinctive means a feature that helps to distinguish a thing; a feature in this regard is a specific truth that distinguishes a denomination from any other. Denomination sounds very close to demon. It is a man-made thing, because we are called to declare the whole counsel of God, not just an isolated truth. Neither is the Church an organization or a religious group. It is the Body of Christ and we are all members of this Body from whom the whole body fitly joined together and compacted by that which every joint supplies, according to the effectual working in the measure of every part, makes increase of the body unto the edifying of itself in love.

I was once conducting a workshop and there was such a strong intense witness to make an altar call to ask people to remove the labels that have been placed on them through ignorance. Great freedom broke out as people renounced their "Pentecostal labels", "Charismatic labels", "Evangelical labels" etc. We are none of these things – we are kings and priests unto God. The moves of God were and are meant to move His Entire Church beyond the Wilderness dimension. No man has the right to claim any movement as their own. These movements were never meant to be for just a few, it was meant for the entire Body of Christ. Those who missed out have some catch-up work to do. Whosoever had stayed behind need to upgrade themselves. They need to study these moves to see what God was doing, and they need to incorporate these truths into their ministries to become relevant and effective in this world. I am so grateful that I could participate in all the major moves of God in the earth. I got saved during the season of the Pentecostal movement, and then had a real blessed and thrilling experience catching the new wave of the Charismatic movement. This was much needed for me because I really felt that there was more to Church life than what I experienced by the Pentecostal ministry group that I attended. I would have gone back to the world if there was nothing more than the old boring routine that I got so used to. Doubtless, repetition kills joy. Wisdom dictates that one should add spice by doing something new. I thank God that He is not a dry boring God – He often does something new. God gets easily bored with the same old songs, which is the reason why we are admonished to **Sing unto Him a new song; play skillfully with a loud noise - Psalm 33:3.**

Anything that we are attached to has an emotional control over us. This explains why many of us get offended when we hear about the things I am writing about here. Please hear me out: I am not writing this to offend anyone. On the contrary, I trust that I am able to help you make some conscious shifts since it is so easy just to float with the stream without thinking consciously about what we do. Unconsciousness controls many in the world today; a conscious shift puts us back in control of our lives and things around us. It is a practice in the business world to question everything being done and to stop doing the things that does not produce any results. We neglect to do this in the Church world, simply because we do not measure time with money. Business people are in business to make money; therefore they question their daily practices. We are in ministry to take more grounds and territory for the kingdom of God. It is more than right that we should also question what we are doing and get rid of some of our religious practices that do not produce any life and visible results. There might also be some old dry songs that have no more life in it that we need to kick out, writing some new vibrant songs so as to create an environment that is dynamic and filled with the life and the power of God.

My dear friend, believe me, we all need people in our lives to push our emotional and psychological buttons to unlock some old energies, so that we can evaluate our spiritual lives and our way of doing things. I was blessed to encounter men of God who dramatically altered my perceptions of the Church, the world and me. It was hard and horrible to let go of some beliefs that I have lived by, which I have been taught during the Pentecostal season of my life. I am so much free now and can actually see that what I was taught was really inaccurate. I had to cancel my flight ticket to heaven and it was very hard because my soul was set on escaping the earth through a so-called rapture. This kind of teachings has blinded my eyes to not see John 17:15 in a proper light. It reads like this and it settles the whole matter of escaping the world. **I (Jesus) pray not that Thou should take** (rapture) **them (the Church) out of the world, but that thou should keep them from the evil.** It really does not matter how evil the world becomes, because the Father has heard Jesus' prayer when He asked the Father to keep us from evil. Evil shall not come near our dwelling, believe it and receive this kingdom of God truth. More and more believers are canceling their flight tickets to heaven. God Almighty has given the earth to the sons of man (Psalm 115: 15). We are here to stay until all the kingdoms of this world become the kingdoms of our Lord, and of His Christ; and we shall reign for ever and ever. This is not a hard thing to God; it only seems hard for the human mind. We only have one life to live, let's live it purposely with the intent of seeing the rule of our Father established in all the nations of the world. This is our inheritance according to Psalm 2: 8. **Ask of Me, and I shall give thee the heathen for thine <u>inheritance</u>, and the uttermost parts of the earth for thy possession.**

Many of us have to make it our duty to call back our energies from inaccurate beliefs that drains us emotionally. Beliefs can either work for you or work against you. Thoughts + emotions + experience = BELIEFS. My daily energy levels has increased dramatically after I have settled the matter in my heart and mind that the Kingdom of God is at hand – it is right here in our midst – it is in us – it is all around us. It is not some place you have to go to. **And when he was demanded of the Pharisees, when the kingdom of God** should come, he answered them and said, **The kingdom of God cometh not with observation: 21 Neither shall they say, Lo here! or, lo there! for, behold, the kingdom of God is within you - Luke 17:20-21.** Jesus also clearly said to us that we should pray for the kingdom of God to come on earth as it is heaven. Religion really makes people mindless. Jesus said it makes the Word of God of no effect in our lives. Scripture talks about growing up, not going up. The more we grow the more control we have over our life circumstances. Have you ever seen a demon being cast out of a person or have you ever cast out a demon? Let's say you did. Do you know that you have actually seen the kingdom of God come into that situation or event? This is exactly what Jesus said: **But if I with the finger of God cast out devils, no doubt the kingdom of God is come upon you - Luke 11:20.** No doubt the kingdom of God is expanding all the time 24/7, because more and more devils are being cast out of people on a daily basis throughout all the nations in the world.

Just read Daniel two that speaks about the stone that has become a mountain and filled the whole earth. That stone speaks about the kingdom of God filling the whole earth with righteousness, peace and joy in Holy Ghost. Praise God! The message of the kingdom of God is a highly energetic message. I have noticed that I grow bigger, more courageous, bolder and stronger every time when I minister the message of the kingdom of God. This message will bring a sudden end to the Church Age and we will enter into the Kingdom Age and see nations getting saved in one day. Can a nation be saved in one day? **Who hath heard such a thing? who hath seen such things? Shall the earth be made to bring forth in one day?** *or* **shall a nation be born at once? for as soon as Zion travailed, she brought forth her children - Isaiah 66:8.** It is time to think BIG! Make God's vision your vision if you have come to the end of your vision. Let your vision give birth to another vision that is bigger than the previous one. **Behold, ye despisers, and wonder, and perish: for I work a work in your days, a work which ye shall**

in no wise believe, though a man declare it unto you - Acts 13:41. Our day to day realities is not the REALITY God intends for us. We should not walk by sight! I am not moved by newspapers or any news cable satellite broadcasting all the negativity in the world – whatever they have to say is mere human experiences that reveals to us that everything that can be shaken will be shaken and that the only things that will remain in the earth is that which is build on Kingdom of God principles. We have received a KINGDOM that cannot be shaken. **Behold, the former things are come to pass, and new things do I declare: before they spring forth I tell you of them. Sing unto the LORD a new song, and his praise from the end of the earth, ye that go down to the sea, and all that is therein; the isles, and the inhabitants thereof - Isaiah 42:9-10.**

ANOTHER TRUTH ABOUT DENOMINATIONS:

Carl Jung once said this, which can be applied to the concept of denomination: The group mind is the lowest form of consciousness because individuals involved in a group action rarely, if ever, accept responsibility for their personal role and action. In fact, unwritten law holds that the leaders accept responsibility, not the followers. This is really what denominations do to God's people. The leaders would resist any truth that seems to contradict what they stand for, not knowing that revelation is progressive; God continually builds on what He has said in the past, which might contradict the truth that they have built on, simply because the denomination-mind thought it was a complete revelation that they received. What was fine for that specific season is now not right anymore, because God has revealed so much more on the subject.

Only few of the leaders are anointed in the denominational group and the followers look up to them to meet their spiritual needs. The people are completely dependent on the leaders to lay hands on them and to pray to get them out of their problems, which never really happens. The key to personal success is responsibility, which simply means personal power, and the key to your anointing is your faithfulness in using your personal power. God will not entrust anyone with an anointing if they do not show themselves faithful with personal power. Any follower that starts to take personal responsibility for their spiritual lives and become anointed in the process becomes a threat to the denominational leadership. This is madness and it has become the root cause for many church splits, because the individual who is growing in the Lord has no place in the group to express him, which lead to frustration that eventually lead to the person breaking away from the group. When we change inwardly, we also begin to outgrow belief patterns and denominational limitations. It is impossible to control people, since truths are everywhere and truth sets people free. God is truth and God is everywhere, which means truth is not found in one location. Truth is also not only found in the Church, because God is not only in the Church. God is omnipresent – He is everywhere, even places where we would not expect Him to be. This is what has upset the Church people during Jesus' days on earth; they were very upset about the people that Jesus associated with. God is everywhere Church! He said, He will pour out His Spirit on all flesh. All flesh, not only Church people flesh!

CHAPTER 8

THE MULTI-PURPOSE CHURCH

Sorry to say, but many of the old-school Evangelical approaches had caused much damage to many believers in the Body of Christ by the way they brought people into the Body of Christ. Many of them said this: "Come to Christ and all your problems will be solved". This message has brought great discouragement to many believers, because Christ does not solve our problems. On the contrary, we have to die to self for Christ to be formed in us to be able to conquer life's difficulties. The real message is learning how to die successfully to conquer your life problems. Many people left when Christ challenged them to take up their cross. We can only conquer in life when we allow Him to conquer us. Many of my problems were a mere setup for me to die to self. Praying for them to be removed or to be solved has introduced me to unanswered prayers. Some mountains have to be climbed over to build inner resolve, strength and capacity in us. God is in the growing business – He spoils no one.

Some other Evangelical approaches have scared people into the Church by preaching the" hell or heaven" message. This message has produced a religious group of people who only attends Church to go to heaven and to escape hell. I do not hereby take lightly the reality of both heaven and hell, but it must be explained within a proper context. These believers have no drive, ambition and motivation to make a difference in their current world – they are waiting for this world to end and for the new to come where they will have no more problems. Nothing can work well when our motive for doing something is wrong. Motivation is a driving force; therefore, we must always make sure that our motives are right to steer us into the right direction in life. Our motives are far more important than the moves we make to survive or get what we want. Understanding is what keeps or upholds us – a wrong understanding has no power to uphold us during hardship or difficult times. There are many of us who serves the Master with a sick heart, simply because a deferred hope makes the heart sick (Proverbs 13: 12). Some of us are just hanging in until Jesus come – we are not really enjoying life because we are not sure what the Church is all about. I have seen too many unhappy Christians in my lifetime and it is also my desire to make a difference in this reality. Not enjoying life is a waste of life. Life is meant to be enjoyed.

I am deeply touched by the infirmities and weaknesses of them who are not really enjoying Church life. I hope I will reach many of them with the message of this book. I know by experience how precious, excited and wonderful life becomes when we truly know and understand the purpose of the Church, even though it might be real hard at times. Happy clappie is a real lie, because clapping hands can't make you happy. You may be happy in Church, but you have some issues at home or at work to deal with.

PURPOSE ONE…

First of all, the Church is not the kingdom of God – the Church is an agent of and a means to the Kingdom of God – we are called to build, expand and establish the kingdom of God, which is to establish the rule of God in all the nations. It is our duty to bring all the nations under the Supreme Government of God. It is the only true Government that can produce righteousness, peace and joy in the entire nations of the earth. This is what every human heart longs for, yet nations are very much unconscious that the kingdom of God is the answer to all problems in the world. God foretold the Israelites when they wanted to have a human government (a king) how they will suffer under the rule of a mere man. Mankind is still suffering today because of that foolish choice.

Adam and Eve were assigned to establish the rule of God in the earth, but they failed to do so because of their disobedience. They were supposed to expand and establish the "Garden of Eden" in all the nations of the world. It is now our assignment. The Church of our Lord Jesus is the place where we are made ready to do kingdom business.

And God blessed the Church (Eph 1: 3 – Gen 1: 28), and God say unto us:
- Be fruitful,
- and multiply,
- and replenish the earth,
- and subdue it:
- and have dominion over the fish of the sea, and over the fowl of the air, and over every living thing that moves upon the earth.

PURPOSE TWO...

We have been assigned to make disciples of all the nations in the world in accordance with Matthew 28: 19-20. Very few ministries are actively involved in fulfilling this important assignment. This has resulted in the Body of Christ becoming weakened because of not making this assignment a priority. Jesus called us to be fishers of men. A fisherman does not only catch fish, they also clean the fish that they catch, which can be likened to making disciples of the believers that has come to salvation. Transforming undisciplined people into disciplined people is as unpleasant as cleaning fish - no wonder why most leaders tend to shy away from this assignment. We would rather fish with no intention of cleaning them. Not cleaning fish causes a bad smell. We have therefore, not yet become a sweet-smelling aroma to the world. Read John 12: 19 and you will see that the whole world was going after Jesus. We do not have this effect; instead, we tend to judge and condemn the world, resulting in the people moving away from us instead of to us.

Making disciples is to nurture the whole person – spirit, soul and body. This means we should help, assist and support people to become disciplined in all eight areas of their human life. The Word of God has this to say about all eight areas of human life, "so that we might walk worthy of the Lord, fully pleasing Him in all things that pertain to life and godliness". Peter says to us that "His divine power has given us all things that pertain to life and godliness through the knowledge of Him who called us by glory and virtue". These are the areas that we need to focus on when we make disciples of all the nations in the world:

- Spiritual needs
- Mental needs
- Emotional needs
- Physical needs (health and fitness)
- Family needs
- Vocational needs
- Financial needs
- Social needs

It is important to mention that healing in all these eight areas should precede the element of discipline. We need both support and challenges. We gain the right to bring discipline into people's lives by our loving support in assisting people to get healed in all eight areas of life. We see according to Luke 13: 32 that cures are a function of the second dimension, which is the second day. **And he said unto them, Go ye, and tell that fox, Behold, I cast out devils, and I do cures**

to day (1ˢᵗ day) and to morrow (2ⁿᵈ day), and the third *day* I shall be perfected Luke 13:32. There is a need for all believers to be healed in all these eight areas of life in order for them to be discipled effectively.

- Receiving Jesus is the starting place of getting spiritually healed.
- We are mentally sick if we are unable to manage our thought life and are being controlled by destructive thought patterns.
- We are emotionally sick if we cannot manage our emotions and are unable to get in touch with our true feelings, which lead to roller coaster emotional experiences.
- Many of us might have sicknesses and diseases that we need to get healed from. This is the kind of healing that the Church has mostly focused on. I still don't know why we did not give attention to the other areas pertaining to life. Being physically unfit is not good for man.
- Some of us need healing in our family life, because of our dysfunctional family background. Dysfunctional behavior is a by-product of low self-esteem and low self-worth, which means, our behavior flows out of our pain, hurt and wounds.
- Some of us have never been promoted in our workplaces, which mean we've been doing the same job for many years, and so we feel very unhappy and dissatisfied in our workplaces. This means you have a need to be healed in your vocational life, which can result in further training and development to prepare yourself for success in this area.
- You are financially sick if you do not have money to spend on yourself; have no extra money to go on a holiday at least once a year; no money to save and invest and to be a blessing to others. You need healing from your financial wounds and you need training to develop your financial IQ. Financial intelligence is the key to your financial success.
- You are socially sick if you can't recall when last you attended neither a party nor have a real good time with your friends,

without being churchy. When last did you meet a new friend which brought much joy, excitement and refreshment into your life? Are you alone most of the time? Most believers need healing in this area of their lives. There is a place for breaking of bread – please don't let every event turn into a breaking of bread session. You are a social being; you need times of relaxation and laughing, which is spiritual without trying to be spiritual.

In conclusion to "all cures", let me say this: You are not completely healed if you cannot make a gratitude connection with your entire bad, painful, hurtful, and negative past life experiences, simply because nothing happens for nothing. All things are designed and ordained to work together for your good. I have so much appreciation for all my bad life experiences, because it has made me what I am today, and without those experiences I would not have the rich life experiences that empowers me now to be effective in what I am called to be and do in this world. I am also very grateful for my sufferings and weaknesses, because it has made me sensitive to the needs and weaknesses of others and cause me to be moved by their infirmities, just like Jesus. **And we know that all things work together for good to them that love God, to them who are the called according to His purpose** (Rom 8:28). Bad things only become good when we are able to see the good in the bad. Negative things shouts at us, positive things need to be diligently searched for.

DISCIPLESHIP STRATEGY:

Identify among your members individuals who are strong, stable, and successful and established in each of these eight areas of human life. Then begin to develop strong teams in each of these areas and let them brain storm and develop a unique workable system as to how they will go about to serve he people of God in all these areas pertaining to their lives. This means there should be eight different teams making a difference in the lives of everyone stepping into the ministry. Let them also develop new teams to reach more people. These team leaders that are already successful in these specific areas can now also begin to increase and multiply their personal success by learning from each others' successes.

PURPOSE THREE...

Discipleship sets the foundation to equip the people for the work of the ministry. This is also not happening, because the person who must do the equipping is doing the work of the ministry. It is like a manager who is doing operational work and thereby neglects his managerial tasks. The manager ought to make sure his workers are equipped to fulfill all operational duties instead of him trying to do the work for them. Jesus assigned five offices to be occupied, called the five fold ministry, which are apostles, prophets, evangelists, pastors and teachers. Their job is to equip the saints, so that the saints can do ministry work in the Body of Christ. This is the work that will eventually produce unity of the faith, and greater insight and understanding of the knowledge of the Son of God, until we all become a perfect man unto the measure of the stature of the fullness of Christ (accurate representation of God in the earth).

We must all submit ourselves completely to the five fold ministry to be equipped and to be build up for what we are supposed to do in the Body of Christ and in the world, and to receive our inheritance. Each of these above mentioned ministry gifts carries with it a dimension of grace that we all need to be build up and to be sanctified to receive our rightful inheritance that will release all the resources necessary to fulfill our purpose in life. **And now, brethren, I commend you to God, and to the word of his grace, which can build you up, and to give you an inheritance among all them which are sanctified - Act 20:32.** Each one of these ministry gifts has the Word of His grace to bring us all into an abundance of grace that is needed to rule and reign in life – see Romans 5: 17.

PURPOSE FOUR…

It is the Church's responsibility to produce righteous leaders to take the lead in all spheres of life. John Maxwell says "everything rises and falls on leadership". There are very few leaders in the world that exist for the sole benefit of people, which is really the foundation for leadership. Leaders do not have to look out for themselves, because success becomes automatic when the focus is to make others become successful. There is a pressing need for righteous leaders to make right what is wrong in the world. It is the Church's responsibility to produce such leaders. This is part of our kingdom assignment, which dictates that we should all become fruitful and multiply to reproduce ourselves in others. Anything that is fruitful has the tendency to multiply and increase with great ease. **When the righteous prospers (rule), the city rejoices - Proverbs 11: 10.**

God has never intended to build and establish His Church on an individual or a family, but on a generation. This is how Paul puts it. **And the things that thou hast heard of me among many witnesses, the same commit thou to faithful men, who shall be able to teach others also - 2Tim 2:2.** The Proverbs writer says to us that it is not that easy to find faithful men, which really makes the process of raising up leaders a challenging task. **Most men will proclaim every one his own goodness: but a faithful man who can find? Pro 20:6** Jesus prayed throughout the night for the Father to show Him faithful men to carry out His work in the earth. It is because of these faithful men (12 apostles) that we now have an account of all the works of Jesus and many of the New Testament Books that gives us incredible wisdom and answers to life's challenges to which the world has no solutions. Jesus is not the answer; we are the answer, because Jesus has already shown us the way. **Because as He (Jesus) is, so are we in this world - 1Jn 4:17b.** You are the answer! Make sure His Words is in you!

Every generation needs fathers to show them the ways of the Lord and to give testimony of all the good the Lord has done. Leaders have the potential to become fathers to their generation. Most of the struggles, problems and sufferings in the world are because of a lack of genuine servanthood leaders. Acts 8: 33 is a very interesting piece to read: **In His humiliation, his judgment was taken away: and who shall declare his generation? For his life is taken from the earth.** Jesus was killed innocently; He did not have a fair trial. His life was taken from the earth, so how can He have children? Nonetheless, He shed His blood and died, which confirms His very own words, saying, "unless the seed dies it cannot bring forth a harvest". The Only Begotten seed died for us, and we are the harvest. We are His children and we represent a new generation that He came to give birth to. This is serious business; we cannot reduce it to something that takes on the form of godliness, but denying the power thereof. This is not a religious game. Judges 2: 10 give an account of a generation that had no fathers, because the former fathers did not reproduce themselves. They did not pass on the baton. It reads like this: **And also all that generation was gathered unto their fathers: and there arose from another generation after them, which knew not the LORD, nor yet the works which he had done for Israel - Judges 2:10.** This was written for our learning.

PURPOSE FIVE

The five-fold ministry gifts are the fullness of the grace of God. This is the grace that makes rich and add no sorrow. The working together of these five graces has the power to produce sons of God that are blameless and harmless, which can again restore the innocence of mankind to shine as lights in a crooked and perverse generation. Producing sons of God is an important work of the Church. Scripture contains that the creature itself also shall be delivered from the bondage of corruption into the glorious liberty of the sons of God. **For we know that the whole creation groans and travails in pain together until now.** There is a deep cry in the world for righteousness, peace and joy. This was and is God's plan and purpose for humanity. We have the power and authority to bring order, righteousness, peace and joy into this world for everyone to taste and see that the Lord our God is a good God.

For this to happen though, we have to be more determined than only wanting to see people attending Church and cell groups. As a training consultant in the business world I had to assess employees to measure their level of competence to be able to take them to the next level. How can we measure our success if we do not assess our people to know where they are? This means we should develop assessment tools to assess believers. We have developed an assessment tool to assess exactly where each person finds himself or herself in all eight areas of life. Our development stages are to take each convert from being a believer to becoming a true disciple and from a disciple to a true son of God; from the outer courts into a holy place lifestyle and ultimately into the Most holy place, which is a place of rulership. This is easier said than done – it is a process that comes with much difficulty, challenges and frustrations, but the outcome is very, very rewarding. The job is done when a person knows how to function under the unction of the Holy Spirit and is being led by the Spirit of God. **For as many as are led by the Spirit of God, they are the sons of God - Rom 8:14.** For we have all received an unction from the Holy One to function effectively and efficiently in this world, which is supposed to be our playground. However, we have been avoiding the world and have been hiding behind the Church walls for too long. It is time to come out from behind the walls and to get into the world, which is the place where we are to rule and reign. **Even so, ye have an unction from the Holy One, and ye know all things - 1 John 2:20.**

PURPOSE SIX...

The Church must busy itself with building a family for God that can begin to flow out into the world to restore the concept of family. Family is what everyone needs and longs for. It is something people can sense, feel and are drawn to. We have worldly people that are members by our Church gymnasium. Some of them have already picked up the strong family spirit among us and are drawn to us because of this. We should never ever forget God's original plan and intent for creating human beings.

The mystery of life has been outsourced to the Book of Genesis – we need to revisit Genesis as often as possible. We are here on earth to represent God, because God wanted a family that looks like Him – He desired from the very beginning for us to rule and reign, which is why He placed us on the earth. A domain can only have one King. The earth is a domain with many territories that provides rulership opportunities for many kings, which are you and I – Read - Revelation 1: 6.

PURPOSE SEVEN...

The Church is a by-product of the life of Christ. Christ is the Prince of life. He exchanged life for death and invested His abundant life in His Body and in life giving principles. King David once said, "Lord, thy precepts or principles give life. Applying principles releases abundant life into our lives. It is the Church's responsibility to teach people life skills, so that they may live life well, with skill being the ability to do something well. Yet, some ministries only focus on spiritual matters. Most of the life skills, management and leadership skills that I have learnt and acquired in life is what I have learnt in the world, because the Church tends to overlook these important things that pertain to life.

Gods' divine power has been given to us for both life and godliness. **According as his divine power hath given unto us all things that pertain unto life and godliness, through the knowledge of him that hath called us to glory and virtue - 2Pe 1:3:** We also see that both Moses and Paul were learned men that received their training and development in the world. **And Moses was learnt in all the wisdom of the Egyptians (world), and was mighty in words and in deeds - Acts 7:22.**

I dare not argue with the fact that Jesus said that the children of this world (unbelievers) are in their generation wiser than the children of light (believers) - Luke 16:8. This simply means, God at times sends some children of light into the world, just like Moses, to go learn from the children of this world. These assigned ones must then come back and teach the children of light how to live effectively in this world. At our local assembly we have reversed this order – our people are now being made ready in the Church to live effectively in the world. Here is a list of some of the important life skills to empower God's people to live more effectively in the world and in the market place.

LIFE SKILLS...

- Management skills
- Leadership skills
- Problem solving skills
- Goal setting and planning skills
- Events organizing skills
- People skills
- Relational skills
- Children-rearing skills
- Communication skills
- Conflict handling skills
- Financial management skills
- Emotional intelligence skills

- Technology and Computer skills
- Budgeting skills
- Sales and marketing skills
- Business skills
- Investing skills
- Intellectual skills
- Training and development skills
- Assessment skills
- Counseling skills
- Life coaching skills
- Life empowerment skills
- Pioneering and entrepreneurial skills
- DVD and movie making skills
- Presentation and lecturing skills, etc.

Life becomes so much enjoyable when we have all the necessary life skills to win in life. Without life skills we simply try to cope with life and is merely existing, having no power to exercise our dominion mandate.

PURPOSE EIGHT...

To create an environment that is safe and a secure, where people can be assisted in their sanctification process. Human beings are always tempted to take the path of least effort, which might cause them to avoid the sanctification process. How many believers do you know have received their inheritance from their heavenly Father? I am sure you would say not many, because I myself have not yet met many believers who are walking in their inheritance. Paul said in Acts 20: 32 that there is an inheritance among them who are sanctified. An unsanctified person cannot be trusted with an inheritance. I am abundantly grateful that the Father personally taught me how to walk the sanctification process and so I was able to walk this process with my leaders, and they are now all stepping one by one into their inheritance. They are also doing a wonderful work in assisting others. The Church is supposed to be a safe environment where people's lives can be nicely sorted out and be set free to become and to do what they are born for. On the contrary, it is a war zone.

PURPOSE NINE...

To also create an environment where people can explore and experiment with their gifts, talents and abilities to discover themselves. "Knowing thy self" is the key to great success. There is a definite relationship between success and knowing yourself. A person that fails in life do not know themselves - they tend to be very uncomfortable in their own skin and their self-worth is very low. We have developed a very practical workshop where people get an opportunity to connect with themselves on a deeper level and be able to look back over their lives and connect with things that they are good at, but failed to give careful attention to those things. We help them put together a purpose, vision, and mission statement to give them a sense of direction and meaning in life. Please use the following list as a guide to get know yourself – we have to work to discover ourselves. It is an exciting journey. Self-knowledge is very empowering, as it promotes choice and action.

SELF-REFLECTIVE QUESTIONS:
- For what purpose am I wired?
- What are my strengths and weaknesses?
- What are my talents and natural abilities?
- What switches on my lights?
- What makes me feel good about myself?
- What are my greatest joys?
- What are the things that make me feel down?
- What is my passion in life?
- What is my temperament make-up or personality type?

- What is my vocational aptitude?
- What is my life calling?
- What is my potential?
- What spiritual gifts do I flow in?
- Do I have a ministerial calling on my life?
- What is my sweet spot in life?
- What is the meaning of my name?
- Am I a right or left brain thinker?
- How do I best receive information – audible, kinaesthetic or visual?
- What kind of negative emotions am I prone to?
- What positive emotions do I experience more frequently?
- What is the level of my emotional capacity?
- What values guides me in my decision-making?
- What is my purpose, vision and mission in life?
- What are the deep desires of my heart? (Desire in Latin means from the Father).

PURPOSE TEN...

The Church is a place of relationship, and the ultimate goal of a relationship is covenanting. God is a covenant God; He therefore expects of us to walk together in a covenant relationship. God works best through a covenant group of people, and He keeps the best of His assignment for such people. We need to make relationships a priority thing in the work we are assigned to do for God. This means we need to teach principles that govern relationships in order for the people to develop authentic relationships. Our life goes where our mind goes. This makes the renewing of the mind a very important thing concerning anything that we want to accomplish in life. Our people need to be renewed in their minds concerning all things that pertain to life and godliness. It is easy to work with people whose minds are renewed. There are many books written about relationships – we must study diligently to show ourselves approved in this world. Make studying a lifestyle.

The Church is filled with people who are much unfilled in the area of relationships simply because they lack knowledge concerning this area of life. It is relationships that give meaning to life. There are five stages in the growth of a relationship, which are forming, honeymoon, storming, norming and performing. Most people never complete this relationship cycle, simply because they don't know about this cycle. Most relationships break down after honeymoon. I have never heard about an everlasting honeymoon. The storm comes to test the relationship. We either pass or fail a test. If we pass, we move on to another level. Alternately, when we fail we will have to redo the test until we pass. People in relationship that overtake their storming phase take their relationship to another level where they discover more of each other and enjoy each other much more.

It is very interesting to note that David and his men had to climb mount Hebron to get to Zion, which was a place of ruling and reigning. Hebron was a taller mountain than Zion. In other words, it was harder to climb Mount Hebron than it was to climb Mount Zion. What is the moral lesson? Ruling and reigning in life is easier than building strong lasting covenant relationships. Hebron means the seat of association, which is a place of cutting covenant. We have to come via Hebron to get to Zion; therefore, unless we prioritize and honour relationships more than accomplishing and achieving things we will by no means have total dominion in the earth. There are still too many covenant breakers in the Church – we got stuck in Hebron and many fell off from the mountain, because of unresolved relational issues and unfinished business.

These are some of the purposes that have burned in my heart that I felt the Lord want me to write about. I am not saying that these are the alpha and omega principles concerning the multi-purposes of the Church. Nonetheless, the Church of our Lord Jesus Christ is the best place to be when you begin to fully understand its purpose.

CHAPTER 9

THE TRUE INTENTION OF A MOVEMENT

Allow me to repeat myself once more. A movement means the act of changing location from one place to another. That is exactly what God did in the wilderness whenever the people moved by the pillar of cloud by day and by the pillar of fire by night. They were moving from one location to another. They were literally moving with God. However, whenever they missed God they were wandering in the same old places. This led to them overstaying themselves in the Wilderness dimension. This is exactly what happens to any ministry group that misses out on a new movement that God releases in the earth to move His Church into another spiritual location. These groups then become outdated and irrelevant in the world. And let me tell you my friend, it is very unpleasant to be around such people. I am not saying this to judge anyone, but such people are very critical, faultfinding, judgmental and out of touch with what are really happening in the Body of Christ and in the world. This can be likened to the very first black screen computers and the colorful updated computer. No one would choose to work on that old black screen computer now.

An old movement is what God has said, which has become part of the history of the Church. History means His-story. God always have a fresh story to tell, a story that would empower His people to live powerfully in the NOW. Faith is always in the NOW, there is therefore no such thing as yesterday's faith. You are not living by faith if you do not have faith for today. **NOW FAITH IS the substance of things hoped for, the evidence of things not seen - Heb 11:1.** We are displeasing to God when we do not live in the now, because it is impossible to please God without faith, which is always in the NOW. To live in the NOW we must do our very best to live in present truth that makes us relevant and effective in the NOW. Present truth is what God is saying NOW. **Wherefore, I will not be negligent to put you always in remembrance of these things, though ye know them, and be established in the present truth - 2Peter 1:12.** Present truth is a proceeding Word from the Throne Room of God, being able to receive it as a result of making the secret place our dwelling place – Psalm 91.

THE POWER OF PRESENT TRUTH:

There are two realities concerning Romans 10: 17. **So then faith comes by hearing, and hearing by the word of God.** The one reality is the faith that we develop through daily meditation and confessions as we speak and hear the Word of God daily. The other reality is to hear a proceeding Word from the Throne Room of God that produces immediate faith that results in miracles as we do the Word that we hear. The voice of God imparts tremendous power in us that gives us a supernatural ability to do what we never otherwise could have done. **The voice of the LORD is powerful; the voice of the LORD is full of majesty - Psalm 29:4.** Power is the ability to make things happen. This is what makes ministries who flows and runs with a new current movement of God powerful. A present truth is filled with tremendous life, grace, energy, power and glory for the sole purpose of establishing a new truth in the Body of Christ and in the earth. This energy wears off once this truth becomes an established truth. The people who benefit most from a new movement are those who catch the wave while it is still fresh, filled with energy, power and glory, with most catching the wave when it begins to wear off. This specific truth then takes much longer to become an established truth in our personal lives, because its energy has worn off. This many times lead to unbelief in the new movement. The best advice in this regard is to stay current and to upgrade yourself daily to stay on the cutting edge. Just watch and see how the current movements are being attacked and how the same people will only get involved after another move has come. I have personally witnessed how the Pentecostals have found fault with all the new charismatic songs, which was a moving away from the old chorus songs to shorter version songs. It was a hard thing for many to move away from the old chorus books and to connect with songs on the overhead projector. Yet, they are now all singing these new fast beat songs.

There are three groups of people when it comes to change. Some people find change to be a very threatening thing and would therefore resist change at all costs. The other group would resist change at the beginning when they hear it for the first time, but they will not totally reject it. They will think about it over and over until they have clarified their understanding. They are the ones who catch the new wave when all the excitement has already worn off. The third group anticipates change, and they are therefore able to perceive that the time for change has come. They are able to discern the times and the seasons and know what needs to be done. These people are the change agents in this world who pioneer and initiate change. They are called entrepreneurs in the world of business. They were called the sons of Issachar in the Old Testament. This is what 1Chronicles 12: 32 has to say about them: **And of the children of Issachar, which were men that had understanding of the times, to know what Israel ought to do.** I cannot overemphasize the importance to identify this tribal group in the Body of Christ and to stay in touch with what they have to say.

Let's carefully study two groups of people in the Bible

who missed out on many of the moves of God in their day and time:

Act 19:1-7 And it came to pass, that, while Apollos was at Corinth, Paul having passed through the upper coasts came to Ephesus: and finding certain disciples, He said unto them, Have ye received the Holy Ghost since ye believed? And they said unto him, We have not so much as heard whether there be any Holy Ghost. And he said unto them, Unto what then were ye baptized? And they said, Unto John's baptism. Then said Paul, John verily baptized with the baptism of repentance, saying unto the people, that they should believe on him which should come after him, that is, on Christ Jesus. When they heard this, they were baptized in the name of the Lord Jesus. And when Paul had laid his hands upon them, the Holy Ghost came on them; and they spake with tongues, and prophesied. And all the men were about twelve.

These groups of people were about twelve. They got saved under the ministry of John the Baptist. They got absolutely stuck in the teaching of John and never moved on with what was happening in the Church world at the time. They missed on many things that happened during their time:

1. They missed out on the Jesus movement and all the teachings of Jesus.
2. The missed on the season of Jesus and the twelve disciples.
3. They also missed on another season of Jesus, the twelve disciples and other seventy – **After these things the Lord**

appointed other seventy also, and sent them two and two before his face into every city and place, whither he himself would come - Luke 10:1.

4. They missed out on the movement of the 12 apostles and the hundred and twenty movement - **And in those days Peter stood up in the midst of the disciples, and said, (the number of names together were about an hundred and twenty,) Acts 1:15**

5. They missed out on the Holy Ghost baptism.

6. It seems like they have also missed out on what was happening on the day of Pentecost.

7. At last, Paul came on the scene long after the 12 apostles and now after all these many years they collided with Paul who laid hands upon them and the Holy Ghost came on them; and they spoke with tongues. What is the moral lesson here: God Almighty can upgrade any group of people, it does not matter how many years you might be behind of what God is doing in the Church and in the world. The only requirement is to be open-minded like the group in Acts 19: 1-7. The mind works like a parachute – it only works when it is open. They heard the new message and were baptized in the Holy Ghost. It is not enough to only listen to the new message; it must be heard and received with a sincere heart that leads to real change and transformation.

A CURRENT MOVE IS NOT MEASURED BY HOW WELL YOU CAN SPEAK OR HOW WELL YOU CAN TEACH THE THINGS OF THE LORD.

It is so easy to be deceived about where you might find yourself in the movements of God in the earth. The Set-man can be a powerful man of God who might be never without words. This does not mean you are current. The gifts of God are irrevocable – He never takes away what He has given us. Being powerful does not mean you are current – you are current because you can discern the times and seasons and you have knowledge about what you ought to do in the given season. Let's read Acts 18: 24-26 and observe a very powerful man of God who was not current in his time:

> Act 18:24-26 And a certain Jew named Apollos, born at Alexandria, an eloquent man, and mighty in the scriptures, came to Ephesus. This man was instructed in the way of the Lord; and being fervent in the spirit, he spake and taught diligently the things of the Lord, knowing only the baptism of John. 26 And he began to speak boldly in the synagogue: whom when Aquila and Priscilla had heard, they took him unto them, and expounded unto him the way of God more perfectly.

APOLLOS' PORTFOLIO:
- An eloquent man,
- Mighty in the scriptures,
- Instructed in the way of the Lord,
- Fervent (being zealous and ardent) in the spirit,
- Spoke and taught diligently the things of the Lord,
- Spoke boldly in the synagogue,
- Knowing only the baptism of John (he was stuck, mighty and powerful in an old move of God).

This is the beauty of the whole story: If our hearts is right with God and with all men, God will always position us to be divinely connected with people who have gone before us to lead us into new paths that would bring increase, life, energy, more power and glory into our lives. This is indeed what a new movement of God brings into our lives. And so, Aquila and Priscilla took Apollos unto them, and expounded unto him the way of God more perfectly. These divine connections will be men outside your fellowship circles, because no one in your circle has the current word in their spirits. There will always be Caleb's and Joshua's in every new generation that would go before us to go spy out the Land or new move of God that is rising on the horizons.

THE HISTORY OF THE MOVES OF GOD:

1. In the 1500 - Protestant Movement
2. In the 1800 - The Holiness / Evangelical movement
3. In the 1900 - The Pentecostal movement
4. In the 1948 - The Latter rain movement
5. In the 1960 - The Charismatic movement
6. In the 1980 – The Prophetic movement
7. In the 1990 – The Apostolic movement

Let's consider what I have previously said: These movements of God was and is meant to move the Church of our Lord Jesus Christ out of the Wilderness into Her Promised Land (a kingdom of God reality on earth, which is an unseen spiritual reality – an extraordinary world that lies beyond human eyes) **But as it is written, Eye hath not seen, nor ear heard, neither have entered into the heart of man, the things which God hath prepared for them that love him. But God hath revealed** *them* **unto us by his Spirit: for the Spirit searches all things, yea, the deep things of God - 1Co 2:9-10.**

So let's make it visual for the sake of greater clarity.

A picture says more than a 1000 words.

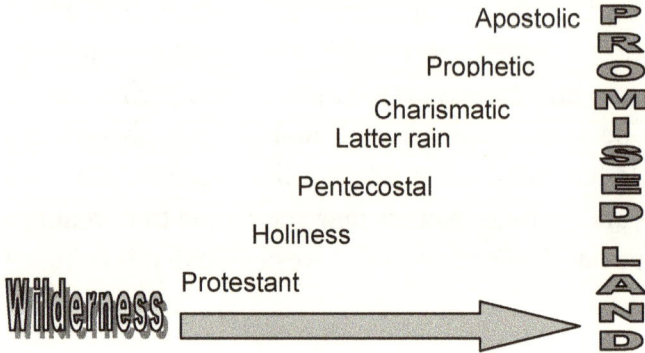

Let's consider another reality concerning the moves of God:

We read in Isaiah 2:2 that the House of God (Church) shall be established in the top of the mountains, which speaks about the visibility of the Church in the last days. **And it shall come to pass in the last days, that the mountain of the LORD'S house shall be established in the top of the mountains, and shall be exalted above the hills; and all nations shall flow unto it.**

I once had a workshop about this concept in a place called Paarl in Cape Town. This place beautifully demonstrates how visible the Church will become in the last days. This place "Paarl" is beautifully surrounded by mountains – it is real breathtaking scenery. The mountains greet you as you come into Paarl. The Lord spoke to me and said to me this is how visible My Church will become in the world, and everyone will be able to see the Church. Nations will flow unto the Church of our Lord Jesus Christ, becoming the prime desire of all nations.

Let us also consider another reality pertaining to the Body of Christ by looking at another picture.

```
                              Apostolic   A   R
                              Prophetic   K   E
                             Charismatic  I   A
                             Latter rain  N   L
                             Pentecostal  G   I
                              Holiness    D   T
CHURCH   Protestant ────────▶            O   Y
                                         M   O
                                         O   N
                                         F   E
                                             A
                                         G   R
                                         O   T
                                         D   H
```

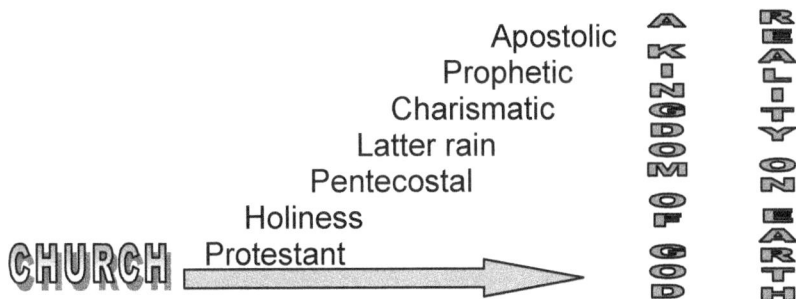

Doubtless to say, there have been some movements that were greatly resisted by the evil one and also by religious groups within the Body of Christ. The prosperity and the blessing message have been greatly resisted by many, even condemning books written about those who have spearheaded this message. Nonetheless, a tree is judged by its fruit. These men were really blessed by God with the revelation of the message of prosperity, abundance and blessings – they and their followers doubtlessly bear the fruit of their message. This message was meant to develop faith that great resources are available for the Body of Christ to finish Her assignment successfully. This implies that we have to go beyond the prosperity and blessing message. Greater priority and focus needs now to be shifted towards our Kingdom Mandate. This has been the heartbeat of the prophetic and apostolic movements in the 1980 and 1990.

Sorry to say, their approach in delivering this message of God's Mandate for the Church was not accepted well, simply because they were too judgmental and critical towards the previous moves and messages that was preached and taught in the Body of Christ. Many of the prophets and apostles also criticized the prosperity and blessing message – People in general respond much better to encouragement than criticism. This resulted in the people resisting these most powerful movements that were intended to move the Church out of the Wilderness into a kingdom of God reality on earth. Many believers have not yet accepted the messages that were delivered by the prophetic and the apostolic movements. God alone knows why we thought that these movements are in competition. The prophetic and the apostolic gifts are the leading ministry gifts that have the grace to bring the other three ministry gifts together to function as a team to make God's dream a reality.

Much repentance needs to be done because of our foolish ways. Repentance is two-fold: We should confess our sins and we should change the way we think. Repentance is the door way to change. We all have criticized some things that we have judged prematurely and we all have said some bad things about God's messengers. The Old Testament people of God have killed God's prophets and messengers; we have done it with our thoughts and with our mouths.

THE 100 YEAR PROPHESIES BY BOB JONES:
What is the Lord doing? Prophet Bob Jones brought a 100 year prophesy for a long time, let's looks at it.

- The 1950's reveal the power of God. William Branham, Oral Roberts, AA Allen.
- The 1960's reveal the Spirit of God. The Holy Spirit invaded the denominations.

- The 1970's reveal the great teachers of God and they began to rise up.
- The 1980's reveal the prophets of God.
- The 1990's reveal the government of God – Restoration of the apostolic ministry gift to the Body of Christ.
- The 2000 would reveal the glory of God. You haven't seen anything yet. Wait till you see the next two years!
- The 2010 would reveal the faith of God. It's not having the faith "in" God, it is to have the faith "of" God. And it's going to be those that have that earring in and hear what God is saying. And what you'll do, you'll proclaim it. And you'll bring it into being.
- The 2020's reveal the rest of God. To where you can rest from your labor and God will work His work through you in your rest and in your peace.
- The 2030's will reveal the family of God.
- 2040's will reveal the kingdom of God.
- 2050's will reveal the sons & daughters of God.
- I only saw till 2060 and the church was still here and it wasn't defeated by any means. It had really grown and looked a lot like Christ. So if you've got short range plans, make long range plans."

This is my prayer: Lord please help me never to miss out on what You are doing in the Church and in the world. Let us all stay alert, sensitive, discerning, willing, and obedient and current with what the Lord is doing in the earth.

Chapter 10

THE THIRD DAY CHURCH

After two days will he revive us: in the third day he will raise us up, and we shall live in His sight- Hosea 6:2

The third day Church is a Church that lives in the most holy place in the sight of God Almighty. Jesus was raised from the dead on the third day and so also will His Church, which He bought with His own blood, be raised up on the third day. We should in no way limit ourselves by thinking that Hosea 6: 2 is only talking about Jesus Christ. This has been one of the ways that we the Church have kept ourselves behind, by thinking that all the prophecies about Jesus was only meant for Him. Jesus is the first born among many; therefore, as He is, so are we in this world (Romans 8: 29; 1John 4: 17b). My beloved, we are heirs according to the promise, and whatever belongs to Jesus belongs to us. **And if ye be Christ's, then are ye Abraham's seed, and heirs according to the promise - Gal 3:29.** We are His Body, He is the Head.

I won't find it a strange thing if anyone who is reading this book might ask who Winston Lucien Daniels is. Who gives him the right to write about a third day Church? Let me first say to you my friend that this book wants to be written; I am simply flowing with the demand that has been placed on my Church experiences, life experiences and working experiences. I know about the "big shot game" that everyone wants to play. I really have no interest in playing that game. All I know is that I was in the wilderness for many, many years, and I suffered greatly in many areas of my life whilst I was submitting myself to a painful sanctification process. I can honestly say that I am a processed man. I am now very comfortable in my own skin, and I got some real deep scars to show you.

Well, I know for sure that I am not in the wilderness anymore; something very good has happened to me. I am in the initial stages of the third day. I mentioned previously that a dimension consists of many levels. We are but only in the beginning stages of this awesome Day of the Lord, which we call the "Third Day". Every bit of experience I had thus far, far exceed what I have ever experienced in the Church dimension, which are a second day experience. This new invisible dimension or higher reality is a faster energy dimension where things get done much quicker. It is a fulfillment of what prophet Amos foresaw many years ago. **Behold, the days come, saith the LORD, that the plowman shall overtake the reaper, and the treader of grapes him that sow seed – Amos 9:13.** I think this vision might have been very disturbing to Amos, because it is a violation of the laws of nature. How can you plant and reap at the same time? This prophetic word is a word of acceleration, meaning that things we used to do in years will get done in months; things we used to do in months will get done in weeks; things we used to do in weeks will get done in days; things we used to in days will get done in hours; things we used to get done in hours will get done in minutes. This might not sound right; nevertheless, the Word of Lord is proven, and it is yes and amen. I believe we should rewrite Amos 9: 13, and it should read like this: **Behold, the days are right here, said the LORD, that the plowman shall overtake the reaper, and the treader of grapes him that sows seed.** Many of us are a transition away from this awesome dimension. Some of us have to travel across two dimensions to get into the third day. We can now all live and dwell in the totality of possibilities in this awesome day of the Lord. My beloved, life is so wonderful in this dimension, all is perfect in this world, and you will always move into greater good from glory to glory, just as by the Spirit of the Lord. Jesus gave us a tip-off, telling us that we can bring a heavenly culture into the earth by praying the Lord's Prayer: "Thy kingdom come, Thy will be done, on earth as it is heaven.

The third Day is a culmination of everything that the Lord has ever done, everything we have been processed in and have experienced over the many years. It is the Church coming into Her fullness. It is a convergence, which is the coming together of all things. I had a personal convergence experience in my life time, which really shifted and changed my whole life in so many wonderful ways. It feels like magic. Doubtless to say, that a personal convergence cannot be compared with what the Lord is busy doing with His Body on the earth. However, you will see in Chapter 11 an overview of the three Days of the Lord, which I have constructed in three columns. The third column gives us a picture of the Third Day. Nevertheless, I will bullet point some aspects of the Third Day and I will also talk about the nature of the first Day Church and the second Day Church.

THE TRUE NATURE OF THE THIRD DAY CHURCH:

- It is a Church that has successfully produced sons of God, that being both male and female. It is now for many decades that we all have heard and witnessed the whole creation groaning and travailing in severe pain, because of all the bondage and corruption taking place in God's wonderful world and creation. We see this in newspapers and on all the different news TV cables in the world. The third Day Church is a Church that has positively responded to this cry by raising up leaders and sons of God to deliver creation from the bondage of corruption, into the glorious liberty of the children of God (Read Romans 8: 21-22).

- It is a Church who does not have a Churchy mindset; they are kingdom-minded and does kingdom business wherever they are located in this world, with the intention to occupy all influential places in the world until Jesus comes back. **And he (Jesus) called His ten servants, and delivered them ten pounds, and said unto them, Occupy till I come - Luke 19:13.** NB! Jesus has now millions of servants in this world. The ten servants were but just a mere sample size of a population, which includes all of us.
- The third Day Church enjoys a kingdom of God reality in a crazy world. It is a Church that has successfully made a transition from a Church dimension into a kingdom dimension. It is very interesting to note that these people are not critical, negative, judgmental, prejudice, faultfinding, religious, petty, and condemning.
- It is a Church that has come into the fullness of the joy of the Lord. All their gatherings are filled with so much joy and laughter that it is like a magnet that pulls people out and in. The unspeakable joy in their gatherings is making their people become stronger and stronger, because the joy of the Lord really makes people strong and powerful.
- The above mentioned ties in with the fact that the Third Day Church has come into the Feast of Tabernacles, which is an everlasting feast.
- It is a Church that the Lord is currently perfecting, because the work of deliverance and all cures are completed in their lives. Yet, at the same time those who come in and have a need of deliverance and healing will get delivered and healed without having to focus on deliverance and healing. It happens automatically in a kingdom of God environment.
- It is a Church that fully understands and comprehend that we have two roles to fulfill in this world, with the one foot planted in the Church, fulfilling its role as priest, and the other foot in the world (market place), fulfilling its role as king. **And hath made us kings and priests unto God and his Father; to**

him *be* glory and dominion for ever and ever. Amen - **Revelation 1:6.**

- It is a Church that walks in the perfect will of God.
- It is a Church that lives and dwell in the Most holy place – they are living in an issue-free-zone. Praise God!
- It is a Church that has made a transition from the anointing-dimension into the glory-dimension. They walk in the glory of God.
- It is a Church that is ruler over much – all resources are at their disposal. Re-source simply means to get back to the Source. Father God is their Resource – He is our Ultimate Inheritance. **His lord said unto him, Well done, *thou good and faithful servant: thou hast been faithful over a few things, I will make thee ruler over many things: enter thou into the joy of thy lord - Mat 25:21.**
- It is a Church that operates under great grace or an abundance of grace.
- This Church is the "House of God" where people can come and be delivered, set free and be healed and made whole and complete, as the church has evolved from being a ministry that focus on being there for the weak, to a FAMILY whose true joy it is to see each member enter into the fullness of life by giving expression to the individual gifts.
- It is a Church that walks in the full authority of our Lord, because everyone in this Church has made Him Lord over all areas of their lives. This is a set standard for everyone joining the House of Alpha & Omega International.

TELL ME, WHO ON EARTH DON'T WANT TO BE PART OF SUCH A CHURCH? IT IS THE PLACE TO BE! SOON AND VERY SOON ALL DISCO'S WILL START RUNNING EMPTY.

THE FIRST DAY CHURCH

This term "First Day Church" might sound quite strange; nevertheless, I define it the first day based on the words of our Lord Jesus Christ, saying, **Go ye, and tell that fox, Behold, I cast out devils, and I do cures to day and to morrow, and the third** *day* **I shall be perfected - Luke 13:32.** The Lord talks about the third day, so it is common sense that "tomorrow" is the second day and "today" is obviously the first day. I trust this is understood and fine with you.

And so we can see that the "first day" focuses on deliverance, this is to say, getting people saved and delivered out of the world and into the Church. **Who hath delivered us from the power of darkness, and hath translated** *us* **into the kingdom of his dear Son - Col 1:13:** Please give careful attention to my wording. I did not say out of the world into the kingdom of God, because that is not what it really is. It is the Church that should get people ready to enter the kingdom of God, which is a reality on earth, not something that is yet to come. Listen to these words of Jesus: **And said, Verily I say unto you, Except ye be converted, and become as little children, ye shall not enter the kingdom of heaven - Matthew 18:3.** Conversion brings you into the Church, but you have to become a little child to enter the kingdom of God reality on earth. A child is taught by parents how to live in this world; you are now born again. However, the greatest majority of us have to be re-taught how to live in this world and in the kingdom of God, as we have been taught inaccurately; therefore, you have to become a child again to be taught. The kingdom of God is God's way of doing things, and as such, we must be taught how God does things. If not, we will die in the wilderness or Church dimension.

The 'first day Church" only focuses on getting people saved – nothing more and nothing less. People are getting saved Sunday after Sunday. However, there is no real focus on getting people healed in all areas that pertain to life. They are only getting people saved and delivered over and over and do their very best to keep people very busy at Church, to protect them from the world until Jesus returns. To make a transition into the second day, the first day Church must begin to focus on getting people healed in all areas pertaining to life and godliness. **According to as his divine power hath given unto us all things that *pertain* unto life and godliness, through the knowledge of him that hath called us to glory and virtue - 2Peter 1:3:**

Secondly, people need to be taught the most neglected message that deals with taking up your cross daily, which deals with dying to self. We must teach our people how to die successfully to self. People are only really ready to hear this message when they have been healed in all areas of their lives. This brings us to the "second day Church". The second day focus is doing all cures, which is to get people healed in areas that pertain to life. Nevertheless, many get stuck in the "second day Church" because the focus remain too long on "self", which are greatly fueled with the "prosperity" message and the "blessing" message. It is the dying to "self" message that will bring people out of the second day. It is more blessed to give than to receive. The highest place in the kingdom of God is to be a blessing; the lowest place is to be blessed.

THE SECOND DAY CHURCH

The message of dying to self is an unpopular message. It is a message that divides, which we tend to relate to as negative. For this reason many Churches do not preach dying to self, because this message will reduce your Church membership. Nevertheless, healthy growth is made up of addition, multiplication, division and subtraction, but most of us only want addition and multiplication growth in our Churches. We prefer quantity above quality. Jesus preached this message of taking up your cross and the multitudes of followers were reduced to twelve men. This kind of growth in ministry is defined as failure in our society. And the multiplication and addition growth by the big Churches where there are only a few members who really take up their crosses, are defined as successful Churches in our society.

Jesus preached a challenging message: **Then said Jesus unto his disciples, If any man will come after Me, let him deny himself, and take up his cross, and follow me. For whosoever will save his life shall lose it: and whosoever will lose his life for my sake shall find it. For what is a man profited, if he shall gain the whole world, and lose his own soul? or what shall a man give in exchange for his soul?- Mat 16:24-26**

Jesus was never impressed with big crowds. **And there went great multitudes with him: and he turned, and said unto them, If any man come to me, and hate not his father, and mother, and wife, and children, and brethren, and sisters, yea, and his own life also, he cannot be my disciple. And whosoever doth not bear his cross, and come after me, cannot be my disciple - Luke 14:25-27.**

LET'S LOOK AT SOME OF THE REACTIONS OF JESUS' FOLLOWERS:
- Many therefore of his disciples, when they had heard *this*, said this is a hard saying; who can hear it? John 6:60
- From that *time* many of his disciples went back, and walked no more with him – John 6:66.

It is a "must" to "test" your members to get an accurate assessment of how successful you are in what you are doing for the Lord. What really counts is not the number of people we count, but the number of people on whom we can really count. The Lord can do far more with a few committed group of people than with many thousands of uncommitted, half-hearted followers. The question is this: Have you ever tested your people to see what is really in them? It is a very unhealthy thing for a minister to be consumed with meeting the Church budget. This kind of thinking will make you gullible to the temptation not to challenge your people, because you are afraid that they will withhold their tithe or leave the Church. Instead, you should seek first the kingdom of God and doing the right thing, and you won't have to worry about what you shall eat, drink and be clothed with, for the Lord will add all these things unto you. This is the naked truth: Potential can only be released through a demand that comes in the form of a severe emotional challenge. It is during these times that we can really see what is in people. Those who leave shows that they were never part of you. They might do better at the place where they really belong. **They went out from us, but they were not of us; for if they had been of us, they would no doubt have continued with us: but they went out, that they might be made manifest that they were not of us - 1John 2:19.** Simon Peter answered differently after the crowd left Jesus. **Then Simon Peter answered him, Lord, to whom shall we go? Thou hast the words of eternal life - John 6:68.** His answer showed that he was truly connected to Jesus. We cannot overlook the reality of Matthew 22:14 **For many are called, but few are chosen.**

Dying to self brings glory to God, because God's glory can only be revealed to dead people who are spiritually alive. We read in John 21:19 Jesus declaring that His death should glorify God, and He said to Peter to follow Him, or His example. We can all replace our names with Peter's name, because we too are followers of Christ. Jesus has set the example of being willing and obedient to the point of death, even the cross. We also read in the Book of Exodus 33: 18 how Moses beseeched God to show him His glory. This was God's reply to Moses' begging: **And he said, Thou cannot see my face: for there shall no man see me, and live - Exodus 33:20.** So the key to seeing God is to die successfully. Christ who is the Rock of Ages provides us an opportunity to die to self and to find our lives in Him. This is what God suggested to Moses if he was really so serious about wanting to see Him: **And the LORD said, Behold, *there is* a place by**

Me, and thou shall stand upon a rock - Exodus 33:21. My beloved, are you making the connection? Did the penny fall in the bucket of your heart? Christ has provided us this awesome place where we can stand in the glory of God. Paul understood this and he made it really very plain in his writing to the Galatians Church. It reads like this: **I am crucified with Christ: nevertheless, I live; yet not I, but Christ lives in me: and the life which I now live in the flesh I live by the faith of the Son of God, who loved me, and gave himself for me - Galatians 2:20.** Self is a law unto itself – we must die to this self, so that we might live unto God. This is the final requirement to make a smooth transition into the third Day of the Lord. We cannot really conquer in life until we allow Christ to conquer the self in us. This is the message that the second day Church should preach and should be supplemented with the message of the kingdom of God reality on earth. Preaching the flying to heaven message can't help people conquer in this world. It is a deferred hope message that makes many people's hearts sick. **Hope deferred maketh the heart sick: but *when* the desire cometh, *it is* a tree of life - Proverbs 13:12.**

CHAPTER 11

THE TRUTH THAT LEADERS MUST FACE

We are all created equally, and we are all equal in the sight of God Almighty, yet we are not all equal in terms of how developed, equipped and empowered we are in this world. Therefore, inasmuch as we are equal, we are not all the same, and therefore cannot be treated the same by God our Creator who knows our personality, competence, character, and strengths and weaknesses. We all have the same amount of time each day, but we do not all make the most of our time. No man is without potential, nevertheless, we do not all maximize our God-given potential equally. And so also do we all have great talent, yet many of us never fully discover and develop the talents we have been given. The Apostle Paul comes to mind as I am writing this. The twelve disciples of Jesus were all greatly blessed, privileged and honored to walk with Him for three full years. Nevertheless, Paul came long after them and after Jesus was already gone to the Father, yet he wrote the most books in the New Testament Bible. There were even some of the twelve apostles that did not write any letter to the Churches. They made no contributions to the Bible, yet they walked with Jesus.

It is very interesting to note that the apostles who walked with Jesus accepted Paul as a leading leader even though he joined the team last. Even Peter said this about Paul, considering the fact that Peter was in Jesus' inner circle: **And account that the longsuffering of our Lord is salvation; even as our beloved brother Paul also according to the wisdom given unto him hath written unto you; As also in all his epistles, speaking in them of these things; in which are some things hard to be understood, which they that are unlearned and unstable wrest, as they do also the other scriptures, unto their own destruction - 2Peter 3:15-16.** Peter hereby acknowledges the fact that Paul had some insight and understanding that they lacked, even though they walked more closely with Jesus while He was on earth. I perceive that Peter was reminded of what Jesus told them. This is what Jesus said to them: **I have yet many things to say unto you, but you cannot bear them now - John 16:12.** Doubtless to say that Peter made a connection that Jesus revealed those things to Paul, and he was therefore open-minded and willing to be instructed by Paul. It is very foolish to perceive when someone knows more than you, but be unwilling to be instructed. The mind works like a parachute, it only works when it is open.

The Proverb writer says, a wise man will hear, and will increase learning; and a man of understanding shall attain unto wise counsels: A wise leader will perceive in his heart when God sends someone into his life to take him to another level or dimension. This kind of sensitivity is life or death. Such moments are a window of opportunity, which might close down on us if we do not act promptly and submit ourselves to the person that has walked into our lives. I will again talk about some of the things in the life of a leader that can set him up to sabotage a life changing opportunity that might never come again. The story about Moses shows the exact opposite of how the apostles and Churches received Paul. So we see according to the writings of the Proverb writer that wise men lay up knowledge, but the mouth of the foolish is near destruction. Instead of listening and learning a fool would speak a lot to try to prove him better. This is the mistake of some leaders when a wiser person is in their company. Moses was learned in all the wisdom of the Egyptians, and he was set aside by God in the wilderness for 40 years looking after sheep, which made him ready by God to lead His people out of Egypt into the Wilderness. Let's now look and see how some of the leaders reacted when Moses came to instruct them in the things of the Lord concerning the Promise God gave them. **This Moses whom they refused, saying, Who made thee a ruler and a judge? The same did God send to be a ruler and a deliverer by the hand of the angel which appeared to him in the bush - Act 7:35.** This is that Moses, which said unto the children of Israel, A prophet shall the Lord your God raise up unto you of your brethren, like unto me; him shall ye hear. These leaders gave Moses a hard time instead of submitting themselves to Moses to be taken to another dimension. **Forsake the foolish, and live; and go in the way of understanding - Proverbs 9:6.** The Lord gave me this chapter after I was close to finishing the writing of this book. I have many times seen leaders walking away from a person that came into their lives who were assigned by God to take them to another level. I have also seen these same men many years later, and it was not surprising to see that they did not make any progress in life. It is so heartbreaking! Well, if it breaks my heart, how much more does it break the heart of the Father? God is not pleased when His leaders do not prosper and succeed in life, simply because they can only take their people as far as they have gone. This is one of the reasons why some people are forced to leave their Churches to go to another Church where people are making progress in life. Can we really blame them? **Let the LORD be magnified, which hath pleasure in the prosperity of his servant - Psalm 35:27b.** Our success and prosperity magnify God; it makes God great, exalted and glorious in the sight of those who behold our lives. Their conceptions of the character of God become elevated. Worldly people do not understand the things of the Spirit of God, but they know how success and prosperity looks like. They can clearly see when a person is stuck or making significant progress in life. **However, the natural man receives not the things of the Spirit of God: for they are foolishness unto him: neither can he know *them*, because they are spiritually discerned - 1Corinthians 2:14.**

Doubtless to say, there are few trendsetters, pioneers and pathfinders in this world. **For though ye have ten thousand instructors in Christ, yet** *have ye* **few fathers: for in Christ Jesus I have begotten you through the gospel - 1Corinthians 4:15.** I once heard a man say this: Why do you want to be an unsuccessful set-man of a Church, if you can be a successful associate pastor? We are not all wired to be forerunners, but we are all wired to run a race that is set before us. I am so glad I have come to know how I am wired, what I am called to be and do, and what I can do extremely well. There is no way that I would want to do anything else, irrespective of how glamorous it might appear. I have found my sweet spot; I am going nowhere else. **Let every man abide in the same calling wherein he was called - 1Corinthians 7:20.** God has called pioneers to go before us; therefore we should follow them whenever we hear a trumpet sound being blown by these men. There are those who are called to be leaders over leaders, which implies that leaders are also subjected to what Hebrew 13: 17 says to us: **Obey them that have the rule over you, and submit yourselves: for they watch for your souls, as they that must give account, that they may do it with joy, and not with grief: for that** *is* **unprofitable for you.** It is hard to lead people who make it difficult for their leaders to lead them. Good leaders are good followers; great leaders are great followers. Our ability to follow other leaders gives us the right to lead others. How well are people following your leadership? The answer to this question is a good indicator of how well you follow other leaders.

WHAT ARE THE THINGS THAT MAKE IT SO HARD FOR LEADERS TO FOLLOW OTHER

LEADERS?

- Insecurity
- Low self-esteem
- Lack of identity and knowledge of your own place in God
- Control addiction (want to be in command)
- Stubbornness and being un-teachable
- Competitiveness
- Comparisons
- Know-it-all kinds of attitude
- Know-better kind of attitude
- Feeling belittled to follow another leader
- Bitter envy (great success by one minister need not excite envy or alienate the confidence and good will of another).

So we see that God always has a Joshua and a Caleb (pioneers) in every generation who would go far ahead of the people to taste the fruit of the Promised Land and then come back to take the rest of us in. Please think deeply about these questions and assess yourself honestly:

- Have you ever come up with something brand new that your generation has not yet seen? Well, we know according to the writings of Solomon that nothing is new under the sun, yet it is new if you have not yet experienced it.
- Were you ever able to perceive that God was doing something new, and you could successfully position your people to ride with that new wave?
- How many successful transitions have you made thus far?
- Can you communicate a vision and mobilize people to get involved without manipulating them?
- Where do you get your messages from that you preach or teach? Is it really the fruit of your intimacy with the Father or do you preach or teach other people's material?
- Do you have the ability to network with others?

- How would you rate your ability to take risk on a scale from one to ten?
- Are you a producer or a consumer? What did you create or design thus far in your lifetime?
- Can you work with difficult people?
- Do you have an ability to raise up other leaders and be secure enough to allow them to become greater than you?
- Have you ever written a book?
- Do you work for money or do you know how to employ money?
- How long does it take you to come out of a hard place or do you need someone to pull you out, or can you say what David said?: I encouraged myself in the Lord. Pioneers have no one to comfort them; they have to learn how to encourage themselves.

These questions are to help you assess whether you are a pathfinder/pioneer. What is your heart really saying when you were reading through these questions? Your heart knows the answer. Those of us who are not pioneers need to pray and ask God to connect us with pioneers to help us stay current. It is mind-blowing as to how fast things are happening in the world – the world is ever changing. To be relevant and effective in this world, we have to upgrade ourselves all the time to stay current. This forces a leader to only focus on at least three to five things that are important to him and to identify first things, making the main thing the main thing. We cannot allow any energy wasters in our lives; it will dilute our effectiveness in this world. We have received an unction from the Holy One to function effectively and efficiently in this world.

WHO'S TAKING YOU BY THE HAND OR WHO ARE YOU TAKING BY THE HAND?

Let us start with Moses. He was called to do a pioneering work for God and His people. God groomed, trained and developed Moses well in Egypt. Scripture contains that Moses was learned in all the wisdom of the Egyptians. God then set him aside in a desert place to go before the people, because his assignment was to lead the people of God through the wilderness. It would not have been possible if Moses did not have any wilderness experiences. Jesus also went into the wilderness to teach us how to deal with temptation, because the Church He was about to birth was going to be a wilderness – read Matthew 4 to learn how to deal with temptation when it comes. Jesus knew exactly what to say to the devil when he tempted him. This spiritual war my friend is about who has the last say. Death and life are in the power of the tongue – we must all learn how to use our tongue to stay alive and well.

The story of Moses is relevant to Churches who are still in the first day. They need a Moses to lead them into a second day experience in the Lord. Chapter nine deals with the third day Church and it also explains in greater depth about the first and second day Church. A first day Church leader needs a second day leader to lead him and to show him the way into the second dimension. Pray and ask God to connect you to such a leader.

JOSHUA AND CALEB

These two men were well able to lead the people into the Promised Land. However, this would not have been possible for them if they had not been in the Promised Land already. They were chosen by God to be part of a team of twelve men who went to go spy the Land that God has promised them. These were Joshua and Caleb's window of opportunity to explore the land and to gain pioneering experiences. Their experience qualified them to lead the people into the Promised Land.

The story of Joshua and Caleb is also relevant to second day leaders that need to lead their people out of the wilderness or Church experience into a kingdom of God reality on earth. They have need of a third day leader that can take them by the hand and show them the way forward into Gods' ultimate plan and purpose for His Church. Pray to God and ask Him to connect you with a third day leader. This is what I can assure you: They are powerful guys, yet very easy going, down to earth and very humble. They are lightly attached to the blessings that God has blessed them with. They do not use God's blessings to belittle His other leaders or make them feel small. I love third day leaders – it is a joy being in their company.

AQUILA AND PRISCILLA

Both Aquila and Priscilla were far ahead of a man called Apollos in the things of God. They met him in Ephesus and while he was talking to the people they heard that this man was not current in the things of the Lord, and so they took him by the hand and expounded unto him the way of God more perfectly. It is obvious according to the scriptures that Apollos was a humble, open-minded and teachable leader, even though he was an eloquent man that was mighty in the scriptures. We should never let our greatness or giftedness stand in our way to remain current and relevant by becoming un-teachable. Jesus had already come and gone, yet Apollos only knew the baptism of John. He was far behind with what God was doing in the Church and in the world. Needless to say, there are a multitude of leaders in this world that has been left behind – they live in an old world that has become obsolete. Read Acts 18: 24-26 in your own time and allow this portion of scripture to minister to your heart.

It is very interesting to note as you read verses 27&28 of Acts 18 that Apollos has made a successful transition to a higher dimension through the leadership of Aquila and Priscilla. His message changed and he was able to show the believers in Achaia, that Jesus was Christ. Apollos became a change agent by assisting many others to make a transition to higher dimensions in the Lord. This is really what it is all about – it is not about us. **And when he (Apollos) was disposed to overtake into Achaia, the brethren wrote, exhorting the disciples to receive him: who, when he was come, helped them much, which had believed through grace: For he mightily convinced the Jews, *and that* publicly, showing by the scriptures that Jesus was Christ - Acts 18:27-28.** Jesus is the real thing of the three dimensions that I am talking about. He is the true tabernacle of God; therefore, His name represents these three dimensions: Jesus the Lamb of God is an outer court dimension; Jesus the Christ represents the second dimension, which is the Holy Place, and Jesus the Lord is His Lordship over our lives; this represent the third dimension, which is the Most Holy Place dimension. **Therefore, let all the house of Israel knows assuredly, that God hath made that same Jesus, whom ye have crucified, both Lord and Christ - Acts 2:36.** Jesus is far more than an innocent Lamb. He is the Christ and He is Lord. The Christ dimension is the second day and the Lord dimension is the third day, in which He will step into this world through His Church to perfect His earthly work.

QUESTIONS TO REFLECT ON:

- In which dimension do you live? Are you still living in the Jesus dimension only, which means you only minister a salvation message, and you are not sure how to lead your people into all the other things that the Lord has before ordained for them?
- Alternatively, are you stuck in the Christ dimension, which is a dimension where Christ needs to be formed in you and your people, but it seems like it is not really happening, since there is still so much strife, competition, selfishness, carnality, envy, jealousy, gossip, etc. among your people? My advice is to pray and to seek for Churches that are successful in bringing their people out of the wilderness. Doubtless to

say it will be a great opportunity and a joy for the third day leader to assist you.

- Alternatively, are you a third day leader who has come into ruling and reigning in life? Trust the Lord for divine connections with second day leaders to help, assist and support them to bring their people out of the wilderness. In this way these second day leaders can begin to look out for first day leaders, just like Apollos did.

We are all brothers and sisters living in different dimensions, which keep us aloof. It is time for us to dwell together in unity in the same dimension, so that the oil that is on Jesus' head may flow on all of us, keeping us all well and alive in a crazy world. Herein will they know that Jesus is in fact the desire of all nations. We are the vessels that would bring to pass what was written in Haggai 2: 7 – **And I will shake all nations, and the desire of all nations shall come: and I will fill this house with glory, saith the LORD of hosts.** Unity movements are not the solution, because we can't walk in unity if we do not dwell in the same dimension. What we really need is the unity of the Spirit, not the spirit of unity. So what is the difference?

Unity of the Spirit is a unity that already exists in the Spirit. This unity is an answer to the prayer that Jesus prayed in John 17: 11 - **And now I am no more in the world, but these are in the world, and I come to thee. Holy Father, keep through thine own name those whom thou hast given me, that they may be one, as we are.** There is unity among them who walk in the Spirit; therefore they do not fulfill the lust of their flesh, resulting in disunity. The spirit of unity is man's attempt to establish unity through their unity movements. This has failed in every city where man attempted to bring about unity, as true unity comes by grace through faith, and not by ourselves, lest any man should boast saying, look what we have done. Walk in the spirit and you will make divine connections with like-minded men who dwell in unity because of present day truth. In other words, remain current and you will not have a disunity problem.

Chapter 12

AN OVERVIEW OF THE THREE DAYS OF THE LORD

Jesus answered them, "Go and tell that fox: 'I am driving out demons and performing cures today and tomorrow, and on the <u>third day</u> I shall finish my work.'- (GNB)

LET'S LOOK AGAIN AND SEE WHAT THE LORD DID IN EACH DAY

1. Today (first day) is the day in which He cast out devils
2. Tomorrow (second day) is the day in which He does **<u>all cures</u>**
3. The third day is the day in which He will finish or perfect His work.

These three days or three thousand years (as one day represents 1000 years) are what God has before ordained, to do an awesome restoration, mind-blowing work in the lives of His people and in all the earth. **For we are His workmanship, created in Christ Jesus unto good works, which God hath before ordained that we should walk in them - Ephesians 2:10.** God is faithful, just and true – He will finish the work that He has started in us. He will perfect us in the 3rd Day. We all tend to shy away from the idea of being perfect, and I am not talking about maturity. There is a weight of responsibility that comes with this word "perfect". How many times have we heard no one is perfect? This is true; no one can be perfect himself or herself, but the Lord can do it. After all, it is He who said, be ye perfect as I am perfect. God can and will perfect us. Just think about a weakness that you had before you got saved. Let's say you are now saved for twenty years, and it is now twenty years since you have last suffered of that specific weakness. I can think of many weaknesses that I have outgrown over the years. I would suggest that we see it for what it really is: The Lord has perfected you in those areas – He will do the same in all other areas of your life. Jesus promised us that He will perfect His work on the third day. This 3rd day is as real as the breath we breathe.

HOW WAS THESE THREE DAYS FULFILLED IN THE LIVES OF THE ISRAELITES?

- Their *today* (first day) was when God delivered them with outstretched arms. He cast out their devil (Pharaoh and the Egyptian armies) **And the LORD brought us forth out of Egypt with a mighty hand, and with an outstretched arm, and with great terribleness, and with signs, and with wonders - Deut 26:8 / Col 1: 13**
- Their **tomorrow** (second day) was in the Wilderness where God cleansed them and healed them to get them ready for the Promised Land.
- Their third day was when He perfected His plan for their lives. **And now the LORD your God hath given rest unto your brethren, as he promised them: therefore now return ye, and get you unto your tents, *and* unto the land of your possession, which Moses the servant of the LORD gave you on the other side Jordan - Joshua 22:4.**

THIS THREE-DIMENSIONAL PROCESS REQUIRES MUCH PATIENCE.

- For all the promises of God in him *are* yea, and in him Amen, unto the glory of God by us - 2Co 1:20.
- For ye have need of patience, that, after ye have done the will of God, ye might receive the promise - Heb 10:36.

SCRIPTURE VERSES THAT SHOWS US THE PATTERN OF THREE:

1John 5:8 And there are three that bear witness in earth, the Spirit, and the water, and the blood: and these three agree in one.

1. Spirit
2. water
3. blood

2TIMOTHY 1:7 FOR GOD HATH NOT GIVEN US THE SPIRIT OF FEAR; BUT OF POWER, AND OF LOVE, AND OF A SOUND MIND.

1. Spirit of power
2. Spirit of love
3. Sound mind - 2 Timothy 1-7 is the antidote for 1 John 2: 16

1JOHN 2:16 FOR ALL THAT *IS* IN THE WORLD, THE LUST OF THE FLESH, AND THE LUST OF THE EYES, AND THE PRIDE OF LIFE, IS NOT OF THE FATHER, BUT IS OF THE WORLD.

1. Lust of the flesh

2. Lust of the eyes
3. Pride of life

These three worldly destructive forces will come to nothing or pass away if we tap into the three forces that God has given us, which is the Spirit of power, the spirit of love and having a sound mind that comes through reading the Bible daily and meditating on His Word.

THERE ARE THREE DIFFERENT GIFTS:
1. Nine gifts of the Holy Spirit (1Cor 12: 4-10)
2. Five fold ministry gifts from Jesus (Ephesians 4: 11)
3. The seven motivational gifts from the Father (Romans 12: 6-8)

1CO 12:28 AND GOD HATH SET SOME IN THE CHURCH, FIRST APOSTLES, SECONDARILY PROPHETS, THIRDLY TEACHERS, AFTER THAT MIRACLES, THEN GIFTS OF HEALINGS, HELPS, GOVERNMENTS, DIVERSITIES OF TONGUES.
These are three vital gifts for the building of the Church.
1. First apostles
2. Secondarily prophets
3. Thirdly teachers.

2CORINTHIANS 13:14 THE GRACE OF THE LORD JESUS CHRIST, AND THE LOVE OF GOD, AND THE COMMUNION OF THE HOLY GHOST, *BE* WITH YOU ALL. AMEN.
1. The grace of the Lord Jesus Christ
2. The love of God
3. The communion of the Holy Ghost

1CORINTHIANS 15:41 THERE IS ONE GLORY OF

THE SUN, AND ANOTHER GLORY OF THE MOON, AND ANOTHER GLORY OF THE STARS: FOR ONE STAR DIFFERS FROM ANOTHER STAR IN GLORY.

1. The glory of the sun
2. The glory of the moon
3. The glory of the stars

THERE ARE THREE FINAL DESTINIES FOR HUMANITY.

1. The furnace of fire (Matt 13: 50)
2. Outer darkness (Matt 8: 12)
3. The fullness of the kingdom of God (Matt 25: 34)

1CORINTHIANS 13:13 AND NOW ABIDES FAITH, HOPE, CHARITY, THESE THREE; BUT THE GREATEST OF THESE *IS* CHARITY.

1. Faith
2. Hope
3. Love (charity)

MATTHEW 6:13B FOR THINE IS THE KINGDOM, AND THE POWER, AND THE GLORY, FOR EVER. AMEN.

1. The kingdom
2. The Power
3. The Glory

ROMANS 12:2 AND BE NOT CONFORMED TO THIS WORLD: BUT BE YE TRANSFORMED BY THE RENEWING OF YOUR MIND, THAT YE MAY PROVE WHAT *IS* THAT GOOD, AND

ACCEPTABLE, AND PERFECT, WILL OF GOD.

1. The will of God is good
2. The will of God is acceptable
3. The will of God is perfect

ROMANS 14:17 FOR THE KINGDOM OF GOD IS NOT MEAT AND DRINK; BUT RIGHTEOUSNESS, AND PEACE, AND JOY IN THE HOLY GHOST.

1. The kingdom of God is righteousness
2. The kingdom of God is peace
3. The kingdom of God is joy in the Holy Ghost.

1JOHN 2:13 I WRITE UNTO YOU, FATHERS, BECAUSE YE HAVE KNOWN HIM *THAT IS* FROM THE BEGINNING. I WRITE UNTO YOU, YOUNG MEN, BECAUSE YE HAVE OVERCOME THE WICKED ONE. I WRITE UNTO YOU, LITTLE CHILDREN, BECAUSE YE HAVE KNOWN THE FATHER.

1. Fathers
2. Young men
3. Little children

1TH 5:23 AND THE VERY GOD OF PEACE SANCTIFY YOU WHOLLY; AND *I PRAY GOD* YOUR WHOLE SPIRIT AND SOUL AND BODY BE PRESERVED BLAMELESS UNTO THE COMING OF OUR LORD JESUS CHRIST.

1. Spirit
2. Soul (mind, will and emotions)
3. Body

MAT 7:7 ASK, AND IT SHALL BE GIVEN YOU; SEEK, AND YE SHALL FIND; KNOCK, AND IT SHALL BE OPENED UNTO YOU.
1. Ask
2. Seek
3. Knock

THE SOUL CONSISTS OF THREE LEVELS:
1. Mind
2. Will
3. Emotions

GOD CREATED THREE REALMS:
1. The heavens
2. The earth
   3. And the sea

THE LIFE OF KING DAVID REVEALED TO US THAT THERE ARE THREE ANOINTINGS. AND HATH MADE US KINGS AND PRIESTS UNTO GOD AND HIS FATHER; TO HIM *BE* GLORY AND DOMINION FOR EVER AND EVER. AMEN - REV 1:6.
1. The anointing when you were first called
2. A priestly anointing
3. Kingly anointing.

JESUS CHRIST OUR LORD AND SAVIOUR WAS:
1. Crucified

2. Buried
3. And He was resurrected

THERE ARE THREE MAJOR FEASTS:

1. Passover
2. Pentecostal
3. Feast of Tabernacles

THE GODHEAD:

1. God the Father
2. God the Son (Jesus)
3. God the Holy Spirit

JOHN 14:6 JESUS SAITH UNTO HIM, I AM THE WAY, THE TRUTH, AND THE LIFE: NO MAN COMETH UNTO THE FATHER, BUT BY ME.

1. Jesus is the way
2. The truth
3. And the life

ACT 2:36 THEREFORE LET ALL THE HOUSE OF ISRAEL KNOW ASSUREDLY, THAT GOD HATH MADE THAT SAME JESUS, WHOM YE HAVE CRUCIFIED, BOTH LORD AND CHRIST.

1. He is Jesus
2. He is the Christ
3. And He is Lord

REV 1:4 JOHN TO THE SEVEN CHURCHES WHICH ARE IN ASIA: GRACE BE UNTO YOU, AND PEACE, FROM HIM WHICH IS, AND WHICH

WAS, AND WHICH IS TO COME; AND FROM THE SEVEN SPIRITS WHICH ARE BEFORE HIS THRONE.

1. Which is
2. Which was
3. Which is to come

ZEC 4:6 THEN HE ANSWERED AND SPAKE UNTO ME, SAYING, THIS *IS* THE WORD OF THE LORD UNTO ZERUBBABEL, SAYING, NOT BY MIGHT, NOR BY POWER, BUT BY MY SPIRIT, SAITH THE LORD OF HOSTS.

1. Not by might (earthly governments)
2. Nor by power (the business world)
3. But by My Spirit (the Church)

PHIL 4:6 BE CAREFUL FOR NOTHING; BUT IN EVERY THING BY PRAYER AND SUPPLICATION WITH THANKSGIVING LET YOUR REQUESTS BE MADE KNOWN UNTO GOD.

1. Prayer – talk to God
2. Supplication - It is the mode of prayer which especially arises from the sense of "need," or "want"
3. Thanksgiving – faith in action

MARK 4:8 AND OTHER FELL ON GOOD GROUND, AND DID YIELD FRUIT THAT SPRANG UP AND INCREASED; AND BROUGHT FORTH, SOME THIRTY, AND SOME SIXTY, AND SOME AN HUNDRED.

1. Some thirty
2. Some Sixty

3. And some hundred

MARK 4:28 FOR THE EARTH BRINGETH FORTH FRUIT OF HERSELF; FIRST THE BLADE, THEN THE EAR, AFTER THAT THE FULL CORN IN THE EAR.

1. First the blade
2. Then the ear
3. Full corn in the ear.

These three dimensional patterns shows us how God works. I trust that you have made a deep connection. My life changed radically after I have made this connection of how God works. Don't be like the masses who are pleased with miracles and signs and wonders only. Moses pressed in to go beyond miracles, signs and wonders. He wanted to know the ways of God, which makes you less dependent on miracles, because understanding His ways causes us to live an abundant life where miracles are a natural part of life and not just to survive. **Ye shall walk in all the ways which the LORD your God hath commanded you, that ye may live, and that it may be well with you, and that ye may prolong your days in the land which ye shall possess - Deut 5:33**

I will elaborate on some of these patterns of three in next few chapters.

FIRST DIMENSION	SECOND DIMENSION	THIRD DIMENSION
1. First Day	Second Day	Third Day
2. Egypt	Wilderness	Promised Land

3. World	Church	Kingdom of God
4. Deliverance	Healing (cures)	Perfection
5. Body	Soul (mind, will, emotions)	Spirit
6. Believer	Disciple	Sons of God
7. Little children	Young men	Fathers
7. Outer courts	Holy Place	Most Holy Place
8. Jesus	Christ	Lord
9. Jesus	Holy Ghost	Father
10. Justify	Sanctify	Glorify
11. 1st Anointing	2nd Anointing	3rd Anointing
12. His Presence	His Power	His Glory
13. His good will	His acceptable will	His perfect will
14. Righteousness	Peace	Joy
15. Passover	Pentecost	Tabernacles
16. Birth	Death	Resurrection
18. Logos	Rhema	Oracles of God
19. Responsibility	Accountability	Authority
20. Faithful with another	Faithful with little	Faithful with much

21 Transition	Positioning	Possessing
22. Promise	Problems	Possessing
23. Measure of grace	Strong grace	Abundance of grace
24. Thy Kingdom	Thy Power	Thy Glory

We can now clearly see in the above columns the characteristics of the three different dimensions. Each dimension consists of various different levels as the Spirit of the Lord takes us from glory to glory. We also see according to scripture that there are different levels of glory. **There is one glory of the sun, and another glory of the moon, and another glory of the stars: for one star differs from another star in glory - 1Co 15:41.**

CHARACTERISTICS OF THE FIRST DAY:

First Day – Egypt (World) – Deliverance – Body – Believer - Little children - Outer courts – Jesus – Justify - 1st Anointing (calling) - His Presence - His good will – Righteousness – Passover – Birth – Logos - Measure of grace Responsibility - Faithfulness with another man's things – Promise

These characteristics are the things we need to process in our lives to get us ready to make a transition into the second day or second dimension. Preparation always precedes opportunity or success. It is possible to go through preparation half-heartedly and then not being up to standard to handle the challenges in the next level or dimension. This we all have experienced in preparing for a test. We will always do well when we are well prepared. Thorough preparation produces boldness and confidence and confidence produces great performance that yields great rewards. The second day or second dimension is a dimension that gets us ready to rule and reign in life. It is a school for ruling where we get trained to reign in life.

CHARACTERISTICS OF THE SECOND DAY:

Second Day – Wilderness (Church) - Healing (cures) - Soul - Disciple - Young man - Holy Place - Christ (Anointing) - Holy Ghost - Sanctify (make holy) - 2nd Anointing (Priestly) - His Power - His acceptable will – Peace - Pentecost – Death - Walk with God – Rhema – Accountability - Faithfulness with little – Positioning – Problems - Strong grace

CHARACTERISTICS OF THE THIRD DAY:

Third Day - Promised Land (Kingdom of God) – Perfection – Spirit - Sons of God – fathers - Most Holy Place – Lord – Father – Glorify - 3rd Anointing (Kingly) - His Glory - His perfect will – Joy - Feasts of Tabernacles – Resurrection - Oracles of God – Authority - Faithfulness with much – Possessing – Abundance of grace or great grace

My goal for this chapter is to provide you an overview of all the things we are meant to experience in each dimension. I know that there are going to be some other things that are going to come to mind after I have launched this book. I trust that the Lord will reveal them to you. The Bible is filled with these patterns of three. This is what the writer of Ecclesiastes says about the power of three: **And if one prevails against him, two shall withstand him; and <u>a threefold cord is not quickly broken</u>** - Ecc 4:12.

Chapter 13a

WALKING THE PROCESSES OF
THE THREE DIMENSIONS

My whole life and my capacity to deal with difficult situations, circumstances and people have increased tremendously with the understanding of these processes. These patterns of three provide practical insight and understanding as to how to walk with God and to go from one level to another, without getting stuck. Some insight might help some readers to get unstuck. Being or getting stuck in life makes life unpleasant and uninteresting. You will also notice that all these different three's that I am teaching on overlaps in many instances, which provides greater insight into the big picture of our Christian life. Each of these chapters starts with a nugget thought on what a process is.

One of the best things that can ever happen to a person is to accept the fact and the reality that life is an ever unfolding process, which automatically makes us all subjected to various processes. Life inevitably becomes easier when we accept the reality that life is hard at times. People who are in for a quick fix make themselves very gullible to unhappiness and much frustration. It is also very possible to get material things quickly and easily, but that only happens to people who have been thoroughly processed and well prepared for life, and it takes much training, development, equipping and empowerment to get you ready to play the game of life. Life is really an adventurous game that we need to prepare ourselves for. Many people are being played by life because they failed to learn the game of life. Some just sit back and watch others who are being played by life and others being great players in life.

FIRST DAY - SECOND DAY - THIRD DAY

The first day is the day in which the Lord starts a good work in the life of a believer. He delivered us from the kingdom of darkness and translated us into His kingdom. We were bought with a price. Therefore you have a new Master, yet the reality is that we still have a programme in our soul, which tempts us to follow the dictates of our old master (Satan). This unrenewed part in us isn't logical – it fires off impulses that destroy logic in favor of strong emotions that is based on wrong thinking. There is therefore a need for us to reprogram our minds with the Word of God to be able to follow the dictates of our new Master. There is an unwinding that must take place for us to become totally free from our old master.

Our old friends are also a link to our old lifestyle and our old master; therefore, Satan use peer pressure to get us back into his world. Unless we break away from our old friends we will continue to be tossed to and fro. We should not try to live two lives – one life in the Church and another life in the world and expect a better life. This is what we call a compromise, which makes a believer a lukewarm person. **So then because thou art lukewarm, and neither cold nor hot, I will spew thee out of my mouth - Rev 3:16.** Have you ever tasted lukewarm coffee, tea or water? Our natural response is to spit it out. Don't be a lukewarm believer. Our first day is a season of total deliverance to be able to make a transition into the second day. Deliverance is the first step towards our healing and wholeness. There are some who by reason of the finished work of the death of Christ on the cross do not see the necessity to undergo a deliverance process. Deliverance is a benefit just like prosperity, so why do Christians not also prosper automatically? Sorry to say, it is not automatic – these benefits must be worked out (Phil 2: 12). Christianity is not a synonym for laziness.

Complete deliverance in the first day sets us up to be healed by God in all areas of our lives, which is what the second day is all about. A transition into the second day is only really possible once we have completely dealt with everything about our past life. A person does not completely become new when he or she accepts Jesus. True change and transformation therefore takes place in the second day, which is the Christ dimension. **Therefore, if any man be in Christ, he is a new creature: old things are passed away; behold, all things are become new – 2Cor 5:17.** The emphasis for change and transformation is to be in the Christ dimension, not in the Jesus dimension. Jesus is a first day dimension, which deals with our salvation and our deliverance. There is really no big difference between an unbeliever and a believer that lives in the first dimension, which are the outer courts or Jesus dimension. The only real difference is Jesus. We have to die to self in order for us to be changed and transformed from glory to glory. **It is a faithful saying: For if we be dead with Him, we shall also live with Him - 2Tim 2:11:** It makes perfect sense for us to die to self; He died for us to be saved and thus, we must also die for Him to be formed in us. He suffered and shed real blood, while we only have to shed emotional blood. His suffering brought Him into the highest place of honor and power. **If we suffer, we shall also reign with Him - 2Tim 2:12a.** As surely as Christ rose again from the dead, so surely shall we rise again; and if we die for Him, we shall surely live again with Him in glory. And this rising again I am talking about is not life after death, for we are destined to rule and reign in our present life (Romans 5: 17), which happens in the third dimension.

We must decrease, so that He may increase in us (John 3:30). This challenges us to grow up in order for Him to show up in us and through us. The way up in the kingdom of God is the way down –

we must decrease in the flesh to increase in all areas that pertain to life and godliness. Writing about this makes me appreciate my willingness to die to self. It was worthwhile, since it brought me into a place of ruling and reigning in life, with negativity having no more power over me. It should be our goal to reach a place in God where we would be able to echo the words of Paul as recorded in Galatians 2: 20, **I am crucified with Christ: nevertheless, I live; yet not I, but Christ lives in me: and the life which I now live in the flesh I live by the faith of the Son of God, who loved me, and gave himself for me.** We frustrate the grace of God if we try to live this Christian life in our own human strength and effort. We should not clothe ourselves with anything that causes sweat (Ezek 44: 18; Rev 1: 6). Sweat stinks! It represents the human strength.

The third dimension is a place of ruling and reigning in life through Christ Jesus, who has been formed in us in the second dimension. For if by one man's offence death reigned by one; much more they which receive abundance of grace and of the gift of righteousness shall reign in life by one, Jesus Christ - Rom 5:17. Hear me saints of God: I have personally witnessed this unfolding process in my ministry life. We are a third day Church that is ruling and reigning in life, and it is such a joy to see people winning in life. It was also painful to see how our people had to die to so many things during our second day. However, it was even more painful to see how some people would not die to certain things that the Lord challenged them to give up, but instead chose to give up by hanging onto the things of the flesh. Giving goes far beyond money – we have to give up something precious to receive a better quality life. The only things that we can't lose are the things we give away. God makes wonderful things happen in the third dimension – things that previously seemed impossible. It is a world of infinite possibilities. This makes our investment in the second day worthwhile.

EGYPT – WILDERNESS – PROMISED LAND

These three dimensions speak of the journey that the Israelites were traveling to take hold of the inheritance the Lord had promised them. Their journey was a natural experience, whereas our journey is a spiritual one. They are therefore serving as a prototype, because whatever they went through is what we experience in the unseen as confirmed in **1Cor 15:46 – Howbeit that was not first, which is spiritual, but that which is natural; and afterward that which is spiritual.**

The Israelites was in bondage in Egypt for 400 years, serving Pharaoh as mere slaves. God heard their cry and brought them out of the land of Egypt with great power, and with a mighty hand. And He brought them through the wilderness forty years. It was really up to them as to how long it took them to go through the wilderness. Their sole responsibility was to cleanse themselves from the negative effects of their slavery in Egypt and to renew their minds with the commandments that Moses gave them, so that they could learn to think like God. God wanted them to be special people above all the other nations; therefore, He did not want the Promised Land to become like Egypt with the ways that they have learnt in Egypt. Thus, this sanctification was a necessity, for as a man thinks, so is he, and as he is, so does everything about him become.

Deuteronomy 8: 2 revealed the purpose of why God led them through the wilderness: **And thou shall remember all the way which the LORD, thy God led thee these forty years in the wilderness, to humble thee, and to prove thee, to know what was in thine heart, whether thou would keep His commandments, or no.** These very same reasons apply to us.

He wanted them to develop a grateful heart by remembering what He has done for them. Gratitude is the best attitude, and it is our attitude that determines what kind of results we get in life. **Giving thanks always for all things unto God and the Father in the**

name of our Lord Jesus Christ - Eph 5:20. Great and wonderful things tend to happen more often to grateful people. Any encounter with an ungrateful person is horrible, and it makes me to realise why God wants us to always give thanks.

He wanted to humble them, because it is the meek that will inherit the earth, and it was His intention for them to inherit the earth. **However, the meek shall inherit the earth (Psalm 37: 11a).**

He wanted to test them or prove them to show them what was in their hearts. Yes, He wanted them to cleanse their heart, so that they would be able to create a better future for themselves. Our issues become our circumstances, unless we cleanse ourselves from it. We are circumstance creators. **Keep thy heart with all diligence; for out of it are the issues of life - Proverbs 4:23.**

The Promised Land was their destiny, but many of them could not enter in because of unbelief. There is a relationship between our esteem and our ability to believe that the best is yet to come while the goings is tough. Any great promise sounds too good to be true for a person with a low esteem. I really do not want to accuse Moses for not giving close attention to the people's self-esteem, self-worth and self-image. I myself suffered from a low self-esteem because of all the many failures, limitations, shortcomings and rejections that I suffered before I got saved. It made perfect sense to me to work on my self-esteem, self-image and self-worth. These people have suffered severely under the oppressive leadership of Pharaoh, no wonder they saw themselves as grasshoppers. This has caused them not to believe the wonderful promise that God gave them through Moses. It is obvious that the people suffered low self-esteem.

DEPENDENCE – INDEPENDENCE – INTERDEPENDENCE

The Church during the Pentecostal days was very ignorant regarding personal development. There was generally a strong perception that personal development was secular. On the contrary, I have personally discovered the tremendous value in personal development and was instructed by the Lord to give attention to personal development at the very beginning of our ministry. I then discovered that people who went through personal development find it much easier to flesh out the Word of God, whereas those without personal development tend to spiritualize everything and has an inability to do the Word. If what we teach cannot be applied in our daily life then I really question whether it is spiritual. Practicality is an outflow of spirituality.

Dependence, independence and interdependence are a progressive unfolding of personhood. The ultimate goal in life is to have an ability to be able to co-work, partner and cooperate effectively with others. It is therefore a necessity to develop the traits of a team player to be able to achieve great things in life. A dream can only be realized through a team. We all need a dream team to go somewhere in life. A team becomes your personal development and self-discovery grounds, affording you the individual the platform to grow in a closed and secure environment.

Our growth process starts with being dependent, which means we all start out not knowing that we do not know many things that pertain to life, until we get to know that we do not know. This leads to a sense of being dependent on others to show us the way forward. The more we learn the more we grow. Growth produces confidence and confidence leads to independence. Independence was a very misunderstood thing among Pentecostal circles. An independent person was normally viewed as a rebellious person, which created a need for such a person to be delivered from a spirit of rebellion. This in fact, has pushed many independent people away from the Church because Church people had an inability to work with independent people. An independent person tends to make the minister feel insecure, as being the only independent person makes him feel in command.

Independence only becomes unhealthy once the independent person thinks he or she has arrived and does not need other members to tell him or her anything, because he or she knows it all. Independence is the middle ground, which are one step away from becoming a mature person through the power called synergy, which is an energy that can produce far more than what one independent person can ever achieve. This is done by working cooperatively with other independent human beings. Our ultimate goal is interdependence. A dependent person can never ever be effective in a team, because of his or her inability to make value adding contributions to the team; simply, because he or she needs others to make things happen for them. Skill, knowledge and experiences are needed to become independent, which is a requirement to be an effective member of a team. Teamwork demands the spirit of cooperation that leads to interdependence.

Interdependence is the key to the corporate anointing that is so much needed to change the world. It is impossible to achieve unity with dependent Churches, which might sound so wrong for a religious mind. There is in fact, a need for independent Churches to come together to share their well developed strength, capacity and experience to reach a point of synergy. Dependent Churches meet to meet their own needs, because they have not yet developed an ability to meet their own needs and to solve their own problems independently. How on earth can they partake in solving world problems if they can't solve personal problems?

Individuals who went through a season of personal development have inner beauty and it is really a pleasure and a joy to work with them. There are many unbelievers that far exceed many believers in terms of their inner ability to work cooperatively with others and to achieve great things. Jesus talked about another sheep that He has that is not yet part of the Church. I have connected with this fold that Jesus is talking about. They have far more practical insight into many of the things that Jesus talks about and they are living far more productive lives than Church people. There is so much that we can learn from them. The truth is, Jesus has two folds at current and they misunderstand each other. We the Church are the fold that is very critical, judgmental and condemning towards this other fold and they on the other hand practice non-judgment seriously. **And other sheep I have, which are not of this fold (Church): them also I must bring, and they shall hear my voice; and there shall be one fold, and one shepherd** (John 10:16). Judge not, that ye be not judged - Mat 7:1.

Chapter 13b

WALKING THE PROCESSES OF
THE THREE DIMENSIONS

A process lesson: A process is God setting up different events, situations, circumstances and people to challenge us to release our potential and to build up our lives line upon line, precept upon precept, here a little and there a little to make us become whole and complete, strong and stable, to represent Him accurately in this world. Let's bring this home by reflecting on the process of learning to drive a car or bicycle and the additional process of obtaining a driving licence. You were willing to go through this strenuous process simply because you had a desire and strong motivation as to why you wanted to have a driver's license. Many of us lack this same kind of desire and strong enough why when it comes to spirituality, all because outer world stuff makes more sense to us. Desire plus a strong enough why makes all things possible.

BELIEVER - DISCIPLE - SONS OF GOD

A believer is simply a person who believes in the name of the

Lord Jesus Christ. **However, as many as received him, to them gave he powers to become the sons of God, even to them that believe on his name - John 1:12:** We have received power to become the sons of God, and this becoming is a process. The sons of God are fully developed, mature believers. They are the ones that the earth is waiting for to be revealed in this world (Romans 8: 19). **We do well to believe that there is one God, but the truth is that devils also believe, and tremble (James 2: 19).** This means we cannot settle down on a believing dimension. We must grow up, since we have received power to undergo the process of becoming sons of God. **Behold what manner of love the Father hath bestowed upon us, that we should be called the sons of God - 1John 3:1-3:** It is an honor to be called the sons of God, with honor being a by-product of how we live and what we have become.

Our next dimension of growth is to become disciples, (disciplined ones) who are people that walk their talk. Please keep in mind what I said last time about dimensions. Dimensions have many levels; therefore we need to grow into many levels of believing pertaining to all aspects of life in order for us to develop the capacity to make a transition into the dimension of becoming disciples. This is the second dimension. It is possible to believe something and not having the necessary discipline to align your life in accordance to what you believe. Jesus clearly said to His disciples, you are **not** my disciples if you do not do what I command you. We must make the connection that there is a dimension that goes beyond believing. In this dimension, we begin to live what we believe, which produces a deeper knowing of the truth we believed in. We now know that we know and no more believing is needed anymore. The life that is in the Word of God is now flowing from your knower.

Jesus' followers consisted of believers, disciples and true sons. The believers were the multitudes that followed Him, because of the many signs and wonders and the bread and fish He provided them. They were the ones who left Jesus when He challenged them to take up their cross. The ones who remained were His true disciples and true sons. Let's consider the heart connections that true disciples make which a mere believer does not yet connect with. Believers have the perception that life consists in the abundance of things (bread and fish) which they possess. However, this is what Peter said after many of Jesus' followers left him. **Then Simon Peter answered him, Lord, to whom shall we go? Thou hast the words of eternal life - John 6:68.** Disciples know and understand that it is not enough to believe, because true life is found in living by the Words of Jesus (see Matthew 7: 26). We deceive ourselves when we hear the Word and fail to do the Word (James 1: 22).

Jesus had seventy disciples, but there were only twelve disciples that were much closer to Him and from the twelve three of them were Jesus' inner circle. This is the conclusion of the matter: The multitudes lived in the outer courts; the twelve lived in the inner courts and three of them entered the Most Holy place in Jesus' life on earth. This is the difference between disciples and the sons of God. Disciples live in the holy place, whereas sons of God live in the holiest place. It is in this place where sons of God are being made blameless and harmless in order for them to shine as lights in the midst of a crooked and perverse generation (Phil 2: 15). Sons become heirs of God through Christ (Gal 4: 4-7). It therefore makes perfect sense why the earth is waiting for the sons of God to be manifested or revealed in this crooked and perverse generation.

CHARACTERISTICS OF THE SONS OF GOD:

- They are led by the Spirit; in other words, they do not live life from their soul dimension. They live life from their spirit-man. For as many as are led by the Spirit of God, they are the sons of God – Romans 8:14.
- They do the will of God – their will and the divine will have become one. For whosoever shall do the will of my Father,

which is in heaven, the same is my brother, and sister, and mother - Mat 12:50.

- They speak the oracles of God - I speak that which I have seen with my Father - John 8:38a:
- They only do what the Father tells them to do. In other words, they do not treat life as an experiment. And ye do that which ye have seen with your Father - John 8:38a.
- They are without rebuke, because they have been properly and completely realigned with the perfect will of God. That ye may be blameless and harmless, the sons of God, without rebuke, in the midst of a crooked and perverse nation - Phil 2:15a.
- They shine as lights in the world – among whom ye shine as lights in the world – Phil 2: 15b; Ye are the light of the world. A city that is set on a hill cannot be hid (Mat 5:14).
- They are heirs of God, which means whatever belongs to Jesus belongs to them. And if a son, then an heir of God through Christ – Galatians 4: 7.
- They minister to the Father in the holiest place. My sons, be not now negligent: for the LORD hath chosen you to stand before him, to serve him, and that ye should minister unto him, and burn incense - 2Ch 29:11. Jesus made us kings and priests according to Revelation 1: 6, and as priests we are assigned to minister to God. There are two types of priests in the Old Testament – the Levi priesthood and the Zadok priesthood. What was the difference between them? The Levi priest served the people and the Zadok priesthood had access to come before God to minister to Him. What kind of priest are you?

The Hebrew writer speaks about the fact that Jesus is not ashamed to call us His brethren and the Book of Romans 8: 29 confirm this by saying that He is the first born among many brethren. **For both He (Jesus) that sanctifies and they who are sanctified (us) are all of one: for which cause he is not ashamed to call them**

brethren - Heb 2:11. It is common sense to conclude that if we do not represent Jesus accurately in this world that it would bring shame on Jesus' name. My dear friend, we can therefore conclude that, these ones that Jesus is not ashamed to call brethren are the sons of God that has successfully completed their second day process, which is a place where we are being sanctified. Unsanctified believers are drama creators, they have a lot of issues and it displeases the Father.

LITTLE CHILDREN - YOUNG MEN - FATHERS

The first dimension is a dimension of babes, children, boys and girls. It is grown up individuals being born again into the kingdom of God and has to undergo the very same process of growing up in the Church as they did growing up in this natural world. Without proper discipling and careful attention a believer might skip important stages and never ever become effective disciples in the kingdom. The lack of discipling in the Church world wide has resulted in many believers getting stuck in the first dimension or first day of their Christian life. First day believers need to master the first principles of the oracles of God, which is the milk of the Word to build up their spiritual bone structure. **As newborn babes, desire the sincere milk of the word, that ye may grow thereby** - 1Peter 2:2: Many believers do not walk with God because their bone structure is too weak; they can only walk to Church Sunday after Sunday with no real evidence of the work of Christ in their lives.

I hereby would like to encourage those who are still in the first day to make it your duty to master the first principles of the oracles of God, which I will put in bullet point for you. Also pray that God would send you someone that can take you by the hand to guide you along this spiritual journey that we all have to travel, to become what we are intended to be and do in this world. This journey will bring you to a city which has foundations, whose builder and Maker is God. This is the place that produces earth shakers, since we have a kingdom that cannot be shaken. You need someone that can travail in the Spirit for you until Christ is formed in you. You will find this person in the second day. **My little children, of whom I travail in birth again until Christ be formed in you** - Galatians 4:19. The key to your transition into the second day or second dimension is to outgrow your stay in the first dimension. This is the same advice that you would give a person who desires a promotion in his workplace. A promotion comes to those who have become bigger than their current job and has already conquered all the challenges in their job. God won't keep you in the same job once you have outgrown all the challenges and obstacles of your current job. Your current job equips you for your next job – this is how we move from glory to glory. For promotion comes neither from the east, nor from the west, nor from the south. **However, God is the judge: he puts down one, and sets up another** - Psalm 75:6-7.

The Hebrew writer got very frustrated with believers who did not grow up after being saved for so many years. He rebuked them saying: **For when for the time ye ought to be teachers, ye have need that one teach you again which *be* the first principles of the oracles of God; and are become such as have need of milk, and not of strong meat** – Heb 5:12. They could not grasp the meaty teaching he gave them and so he said this to them. **For every one that uses milk *is* unskillful in the word of righteousness: for he is a babe** - Heb 5:13. Can you imagine giving a baby meat to eat? A babe would choke himself to death as babies can only drink milk. To grow up in the kingdom of God we need to go beyond teachings that contain milk only. **But strong meat belongs to them that are of full age, *even* those who by reason of use have their senses exercised to discern both good and evil** - Heb 5:14. We are called to shine as lights in a crazy world – we therefore need to be able to discern both good and evil to be able to shine as lights in a crooked and perverse generation.

FIRST PRINCIPLES:

Hebrews 6: 1-2

- Repentance from dead works
- Faith toward God
- Doctrine of baptisms
- Laying on of hands
- Resurrection of the dead
- Eternal judgment

Let's read what Apostle John has to say about little children, young men and fathers:

- 1John 2:1 My little children, these things write I unto you, that ye sin not. And if any man sin, we have an advocate with the Father, Jesus Christ the righteous:

- 1Jn 2:12 I write unto you, little children, because your sins are forgiven you for his name's sake.

- 1Jn 2:13 I write unto you, fathers, because ye have known him *that is* from the beginning. I write unto you, young men, because ye have overcome the wicked one. I write unto you, little children, because ye have known the Father.

- 1Jn 2:14 I have written unto you, fathers, because ye have known him *that is* from the beginning. I have written unto you, young men, because ye are strong, and the word of God abides in you, and ye have overcome the wicked one.

CHAPTER 13c

WALKING THE PROCESSES OF
THE THREE DIMENSIONS

A process lesson: A process is very much psychological – it is the performance of some composite cognitive activity; an operation that affects mental contents; "the process of thinking", according to the dictionary book. That's why it is so tempting to quit a process – process is really very intense at times. Process is a life-giving entity even though it does not feel so while we are in it. It is a lie to think that you are losing your life even though it feels so at times. The truth is, we are losing the things that produce death in our lives in exchange for the life giving principles that we learn and embrace. The life-giving principle in your heart is the thing that produces new life. Process is therefore the key to lasting success – it is possible to get quick success by skipping processes, but it is not lasting.

JUSTIFY - SANCTIFY - GLORIFY

It is impossible for anyone not to notice us wherever we go in this world, if we have been sanctified by the Lord. No doubt sanctification is very painful and unbearable at times, but God's grace upholds us and empowers us to make it to the end. The first dimension deals with total justification concerning all areas of our lives which, in reality, set us up to move to the second dimension where we are sanctified in all areas of our lives. Glorification is what happens to us, it is not something we need to make happen.

God had all the reason and adequate ground to assert a claim against us for our sinful life and unrighteousness. **For the wages of sin is death** - Romans 6:23a. However, He found it in His heart to offer up His Son to die in our stead – this is called the gift of God. **But the gift of God is eternal life through Jesus Christ our Lord** - Romans 6:23b. We have been let off the hook and His blood provides us proof of justification. He has absolved us from the responsibility of our evil ways. This to me is mind-blowing. We have nothing to give to Him to make up for what He has done for us. The only thing we can do is to present our bodies a living sacrifice, holy, acceptable unto God, which is our reasonable service. The reality of being justified must be translated into all areas and every facet of our lives, so that there would not be anything that the evil one can use against us to condemn us. Many of us have failed to do exactly this. Therefore, we struggle to die successfully to self, which is an intense emotional demand that the sanctification process places on all of us. The wilderness (Church) which is the place of sanctification has become hell on earth for many of us, because we have not allowed ourselves to be justified in all areas that pertain to life, even though the work was completed when Christ said "it is finish" when He died on the cross. There is far too much sin-consciousness in the Body of Christ. I wish we all would know, understand and appreciate the power of consciousness, that whatever we are conscious of, we manifest in our external world. I beseech you therefore, by the mercies of God, to meditate on Hebrew 9: 14 until you are fully convinced and persuaded that all your sins have been forgiven and that sin has no more power over you. **How much more shall the blood of Christ, who through the eternal Spirit offered himself without spot to God, purge your conscience from dead works to serve the living God?** I exhort you to have dominion over sin in Jesus' name. Don't settle for anything less!

The above mentioned is necessary to make a transition into the second dimension, which is the Church dimension that represents our spiritual wilderness. The purpose of the wilderness can be best explained by reading through a few different Bible versions of what Deuteronomy 8: 16 says about the purpose of the wilderness dimension (Church dimension).

- He also gave you manna, a kind of food your ancestors had never even heard about. The LORD was testing you to make you trust him, so that later on he could be good to you - (CEV).
- Who fed you in the wilderness with manna that your fathers did not know, that he might humble you and test you, to do you good in the end - (ESV).
- In the desert he gave you manna to eat, food that your ancestors had never eaten. He sent hardships on you to test you, so that in the end he could bless you with good things - (GNB).
- He was the one who fed you in the desert with manna, which your ancestors had never seen. He did this in order to humble you and test you. But he also did this so that things would go well for you in the end - (GW).
- The God who gave you manna to eat in the wilderness, something your ancestors had never heard of, in order to give you a taste of the hard life, to test you so that you would be prepared to live well in the days ahead of you - (MSG).

Always keep in mind that every sermon that you hear in Church is in fact, the Lord who is giving you manna to eat. **However, he answered and said, It is written, Man shall not live by bread alone, but by every word that proceeds out of the mouth of God** - Matt 4:4. Furthermore, be mindful that you are going to be tested on every sermon that you hear, because the enemy comes for the Word's (manna) sake according to Mark 4: 17. This test is to humble you and to show you what is in your heart. Jesus Himself was tested in the wilderness – see Matthew 4. All of these happenings are to sanctify us to render us holy by affliction, trials, tribulation, hardship and difficulties. **Knowing this, that the trying of your faith works at patience (character development)** - James 1:3. Christ who is the hope of glory in us gets squeezed out of us under severe pressure - **For our light affliction, which is but for a moment, works for us a far more exceeding and eternal weight of glory** - 2Corithians 4:17. This is what the sanctification process is all about. It is therefore best to count it all joy when we fall into various trials and all sorts of hardship and difficulties, with the knowing and understanding that it is not unto death but for the glory of God to be revealed in us and through us.

Blows that hurt cleanses away evil and so do stripes the inner depths of our heart. My dear friend, the sanctification process removes impurities from our minds and heart. This vital process cleanses us from all the mess and junk from our past and empowers us to live in the now, which is the gateway to our future. Whoever He justifies, He also glorifies, but the truth of the matter is, there can be no glorification without sanctification. Glory does not hurt; it blesses and makes you shine! **Let your light so shine before men, that they may see your good works, and glorify your Father, which is in heaven** - Matthew 5:16. Our Father gets the glory when we are being glorified.

RIGHTEOUSNESS - PEACE - JOY

Righteousness is the most precious gift to mankind – it is a divine supernatural ability to adhere to moral principles, which leads to peace and joy in the Holy Ghost. That is what the kingdom of God is all about. **For the kingdom of God are not meat and drink; but righteousness, and peace, and joy in the Holy Ghost** (Romans 14:17). Right living produces peace; doing the wrong thing produces a lack of peace, which is really a horrible feeling. Repentance is the only way of escape out of this horrible feeling. It really pays to live right.

Righteousness, peace and joy are dimensions of the kingdom of God. It is very possible to be righteous and still only experience peace occasionally. Those who bear the fruits of righteousness constantly live in a state of peace and joy in the Holy Ghost, which implies that they fully live in the kingdom of God on the earth. The "kingdom of God" as it is in heaven is an absolute reality in their lives on the earth. I am reminded of a season in my life that I have experienced absolute peace for a long time, nothing in this world could disturb my peace; it felt like magic. At the time, I was unaware that I was in fact, enjoying a second dimension of the kingdom of God. Jesus taught us to pray like this, **"Thy kingdom come, Thy will be done in earth, as it is in heaven** - Matt 6:10. Growing up is the key to enjoying kingdom life on earth. It is very possible for anyone of us to enjoy a real sense of rightness, peace and joy in a crazy world.

A gift is something we receive – it is not something we work for. **For He hath made Him to be sin for us, who knew no sin; that we might be made the righteousness of God in Him** - 2Cor 5:21. We are not saved by good works, but we are saved unto good works (Eph 2: 8). This implies that we receive our righteousness, but there are righteous works we need to do to be able to bear the fruit of righteousness, which is peace and joy in the Holy Ghost. Fruit is the result of labour; though not labour in the flesh but inspired works. Righteousness also means "virtue, integrity," a faithful discharge of all the duties which we owe to God or to our fellow-man. NB! A righteous man is not a man without sin and also not a man whose whole attention is absorbed by the mere ceremonies and outward forms of religion (1John 1: 8; 2Tim 3: 5).

RESPONSIBILITY - ACCOUNTABILITY - AUTHORITY.

This is a process of growing up into our given authority. **All power and authority in heaven and in earth has been given to Jesus Christ according to Matthew 28: 18**, and this very same power and authority Jesus delegated unto us. Delegate means to transfer power to someone or assign a task to a person. This is exactly what Jesus did – He gave us power and an assignment to make disciples of all nations. This is a high responsibility. It means we have been given power to exercise control over nations, which includes the power or right to give orders and take decisions. This also means your views concerning important issues that pertain to life are been taken as definitive. We need to grow into this kind of authority through responsibility and by being accountable. We are liable to account for our actions regarding the assignment that Jesus has given us.

Accountability means we are fully accountable for our day to day action. A person with authority has felt-influence – they are absolutely free from doubt; they believe in themselves and in their abilities, and they speak with great certainty and authority. We are called to be a force for good in our society. However, there are few believers that walk in this kind of authority – the authority that has been given to them lies dormant because of a lack of responsibility and accountability. It does not matter how much parents loves their kids, they will not give them their car key, unless they have proven themselves to be responsible and accountable. We cannot expect anything less from God Almighty.

People in general shy away from taking full responsibility for the consequences of all their actions. This started in the Garden of Eden when Adam and Eve failed to take full responsibility for their sinful action (disobedience); instead they blamed and accused each other for eating the forbidden fruit. They hid themselves away instead of being transparent to come clean. This has become a common thing to mankind – we blame and accuse each other for the consequences of our action. In reality, we are giving away our power every time when we blame and accuse. Learning to take responsibility is our training grounds for how to handle authority when we receive it. We cannot be trusted with authority if we cannot be trusted with personal power (responsibility). The path to great authority is to claim responsibility for every single incident and for everything that is happening in your life, however trivial and irrespective of who is right or wrong. This is what it takes to build capacity to be able to learn to be accountable for those who are placed over us. Faithfulness in taking responsibility and being accountable produces authority in the kingdom of God. We are being trained to be responsible in the first dimension (outer courts) and to exercise accountability in the second dimension (holy place). Authority thus, is what we receive in the third dimension (most holy place), which is a place of ruling and reigning in life.

CHAPTER 13D

WALKING THE PROCESSES OF
THE THREE DIMENSIONS

A process lesson: A process is a particular course of action intended to achieve a result, for example, "the procedure of obtaining a driver license"; "it was a process of trial and error". A process is unseen, but it is surer than the things we can see with our natural eyes. Learn to trust the process....

FIRST DIMENSION FAITHFULNESS - SECOND DIMENSION FAITHFULNESS - THIRD DIMENSION FAITHFULNESS.

The first dimension of faithfulness is to be faithful with another man's thing; the second dimension is faithfulness with little and the third dimension is faithfulness with much. There are indeed levels and dimensions of faithfulness. It is our highest levels and dimensions of faithfulness that will cause us to abound in blessings that can last for many generations. A faithful man shall abound with blessings - Proverbs 28:20a. It is our responsibility to leave an inheritance for our children's children – the Word of God calls a person who are able to leave an inheritance to his children's children a good man (Proverbs 13: 22). What do we call a person who is unable to leave an inheritance to his children's children? (Self-reflection)

The workings of God are no different from how wise parents brought up their children. I am saying wise, because many parents have no real knowledge of how to raise their kids in the ways of the Lord. A child has nothing of his own when he stays with his parents – it is a parent's responsibility to teach them how to manage and handle their resources faithfully. This prepares the child for his or her own things. God's promotion is always based on our faithfulness; therefore, God also first entrusted us with other people's stuff to learn faithfulness from them. **And if ye have not been faithful in that which is another man's, who shall He give you that which is your own?** (Luke 16:12). Faithfulness in another man's thing is measured by how well we treat and handle other people things. We ought to treat other people's stuff as if it is our very own. The Lord will give us our own if we can do this consistently for long seasons.

We should not despise small beginnings, because in it lays the seed for greatness and greater things. We should always appreciate the least of what we have been entrusted with. A man that shows fidelity in small matters will also in large; and he that will cheat and defraud in little things will also do the same in much. Faithfulness is best on trust and responsibility. Fidelity is required in small matters as well as in those of more importance. **He that is faithful in that which is least is faithful also in much: and he that is unjust in the least is unjust also in much** (Luke 16:10).

We learn management skills when we exercise faithfulness over small things. Management entails planning, organizing, prioritizing, keeping record and keeping account over things. This gives us capacity to handle more and more things. There are ranks of management. **His lord said unto him, Well done, thou good and faithful servant: thou hast been faithful over a few things, I will make thee ruler over many things: enter thou into the joy of thy lord** (Matt 25:21). Ruler over much speaks of leadership capacity, which is an ability to provide oversight over everything. Management plus leadership equals great capacity. A CEO (leadership) is accountable for the entire business. A manager is only held accountable for a department, which is a small part of the entire business. God is calling His people to become world leaders, so that they might be rulers over everything that He has created for our enjoyment and pleasure. God has given us all things richly to enjoy (1Tim 6: 17). Life is meant to be enjoyed.

THIS IS THE CONCLUSION OF THE MATTER:

FIRST DIMENSION FAITHFULNESS – learning faithfulness by being entrusted with other people's things.

SECOND DIMENSION FAITHFULNESS – learning to be faithful and grateful with the little that we have been entrusted with.

THIRD DIMENSION FAITHFULNESS – learning to be faithful over much and never to become corrupt and arrogant.

TRANSTION - POSITIONING - POSSESSING

Always keep this in mind: God is dynamic, not static. He is forever on the move to change and transform the earth into what He has intended it to be from the beginning, which was reflected in the Garden of Eden. He is once again making the earth to become like the Garden of Eden; therefore, He is constantly releasing new and fresh revelation to upgrade our minds, because we become what we think. An upgraded mind leads to consistent progression because our lives go where our minds go. A transition is a movement from one level to another level or from one dimension to another dimension. There is always a period of dryness that gives us an indication that it is time to make another transition. This is not a once off experience. God is perfect. Therefore, He does not change, and He is challenging us to be perfect just like Him. Therefore, we are constantly under construction as He takes us from glory to glory to an ever-increasing glory.

The only real permanent thing in life is change, and a transition will always be stormy if we did not anticipate and prepare ourselves for change. This means we have to reposition ourselves to align with present or current truth, so that we can be ready for what need to take place in our lives. For instance, there are some things we need to let go of or some friends that we need to move away from, because some relationships are seasonal and many other readjustments that we need to make; or we have to restructure our entire lives to be able to possess what God has in-store for us. Whatever God has in-store for us will advance our cause in life, which will enable us to do more to establish the kingdom of God on the earth. This pattern my friend is an ongoing thing – learn to live with it and be wise to sharpen your ability to make smooth transitions that will take you from glory to glory. Be also wise not to get attached to things – be lightly attached to anything with the knowing that in life we own nothing. We are stewards of whatever has been placed in our possession. People who derive their identity from what they possess usually struggle to make transitions. Furthermore, keep in mind that borrowed strength creates weakness. Therefore, never borrow strength from what you have; from your position or title or anything else that makes you look smart. **And he said unto them, Take heed, and beware of covetousness: for a man's life consisteth not in the abundance of the things which he possessed** (Luke 12:15).

PROMISE - PROBLEM - POSSSESING

The Israelites received the promise of the Promised Land when they were in Egypt, which was their first dimension. Anyone who has ever received a wonderful prophetic word knows what happens after one receives such a prophetic word. All hell seems to break lose and your whole life seems to go into the opposite direction of the wonderful prophetic word that you have received. Simply, because affliction or persecution always arises for the word's sake (Mark 4: 17).

For the Israelites, this led to the second dimension called the problem stage, which was their wilderness. The purpose of the wilderness was to process them to get them ready for the fulfillment of their promise. **Having therefore, these promises, dearly beloved, let us cleanse ourselves from all filthiness of the flesh and spirit, perfecting holiness in the fear of God** (2Co 7:1). Sanctification always precedes the fulfillment of any promise from God.

All the promises of God in Him are yea, and in Him amen, unto the glory of God by us (2Cor 1: 20). God does not work independently from us – we have a role to play for the promises of God to be fulfilled in our lives, as we are called to be co-workers and partakers (partners) with God. Secondly, the fulfillment of all the promises which God has made to His people will result in His glory and praise. The fact that He has made such promises is an act that tends to His own glory, since it was of His mere grace that they were made. The fulfillment of God's promises in our lives also tends to produce elevated views of His fidelity and goodness. You see, Hebrew 6: 12 tells us that it is through faith and patience that we inherit (possess) the promises of God. Why? For God value our character development far more than our happiness.

This very same pattern applies to God's New Testament people. God remains the same yesterday, today and forever. Everything we need, want or desire is in the kingdom of God, and we enter this dimension through many trials and tribulation (Acts 14: 22b); the Church dimension is our wilderness. It might now make sense to you why there are so many problems in the Church. All the problems we may ever encounter in the Church are meant to process us and to make us better, not bitter. The way we see a problem is many times the problem. A problem must be converted into an assignment that needs to be carried out by those who have been confronted by the problem. There is a solution for every single problem in this world. We are part of the problem if we do not have the solution. The greatest business opportunities come through problems that want to be solved. This pattern: **promise - problem and possession** is an ongoing spiritual experience, because there are thousands of God's promises that we need to possess in our lifetime. It is not an event like the Israelites, who had a single Promised Land. We have thousands upon thousands of promises to possess in our lifetime. **For all the promises of God in him are yea, and in him Amen, unto the glory of God by us** (2Cor 1:20). Please put your heart and mind in a higher gear to possess every promise that God has for you. Learn to get excited about problems instead of becoming negative and complain about what is wrong. Keep this in mind: Never think on why things cannot be done; think on why it can be done.

MEASURE OF GRACE - STRONG GRACE - ABUNDANCE OF GRACE

We all started out with a small measure of grace. **However, unto every one of us is given grace according to the measure of the gift of Christ** (Eph 4:7). It is our faithfulness, diligence and consistency in developing and exercising the many gifts that the Lord has given us that determines how far we grow in grace. Peter tells us in 2Pet 3: 18a **to grow in grace.** We grow in grace when we exercise our gifts by being a blessing to others through service. Jesus also told us that serving others will make us become great in the kingdom (Matt 23: 11). This means anyone can become great, because anyone can serve. We grow strong in grace when we live to serve others, as the purpose of strength is to serve the weak. Too many of us wait to be served, and so we never grow in grace and remain stuck in the dimension of a measure of grace. This results in many of our needs not being met.

Listen what Paul said about the grace of our Lord Jesus Christ – see 2Co 8:9: **For ye know the grace of our Lord Jesus Christ, that, though he was rich, yet for your sakes, he became poor, that ye through his poverty might be rich.** The grace of our

Lord Jesus Christ is supposed to make us rich, and I beg you not to be religious to think that rich only means spiritual riches, and not to be materialistic to think that rich means only natural things like money. However, it is very obvious that many of our brothers and sisters have become extremely financially rich because of the great grace on their lives. They have been a blessing to many by laying down their lives through much service to humanity. We cannot become rich with a measure of grace or strong grace – we need great grace or an abundance of grace to reign in life (Rom 5: 17). Doubtless a measure of grace meets some of our needs and strong grace makes a believer becomes prosperous, but it takes great grace to become rich and great in the earth. Scripture proofs to us that the believers that were related to the early day apostles did not lack any good thing, because of the great grace that was on the apostles. **And with great power gave the apostles witness of the resurrection of the Lord Jesus: and great grace (abundance of grace) was upon them all. Neither was there any among them that lacked** (Act 4:33-34a).

I personally have witnessed over the many years needy ministries, strong ministries where people prosper and ministries where people become rich, because of great grace. This is determined by the level of grace in that specific house where you fellowship. The great grace in a house is what is on the set man of the house. We can't take people where we have never been, neither can we give what we do not possess.

THERE IS A MEASURE OF GRACE...
But unto every one of us is given grace according to the measure of the gift of Christ - Eph 4:7.

AND THERE IS STRONG GRACE...

Thou, therefore, my son, be strong in the grace that is in Christ Jesus- 2Tim 2:1.

AND THERE IS GREAT GRACE OR AN ABUNDANCE OF GRACE...

And with great power gave the apostle's witness of the resurrection of the Lord Jesus: and great grace (abundance of grace) was upon them all.

For if by one man's offence death reigned by one; much more they which receive abundance of grace (great grace) and of the gift of righteousness shall reign in life by one, Jesus Christ - Rom 5:17.

God releases great wealth for a great cause, and it takes great grace to do a great work for God and humanity. Things really happen very quickly in Houses where there is strong grace and even much quicker where there is great grace. A House of great grace is where everyone gets encouraged to discover their calling, gifts, abilities and talents to serve each other and their communities and ultimately, the nations.

THY KINGDOM - THY POWER - THY GLORY

For Thine is the kingdom, and the power, and the glory, for ever. Amen - Matthew 6:13b. This verse shows us a progression concerning the kingdom of God, which are dimensions of God's kingdom. The King of the kingdom will never entrust anyone with kingdom power, unless they are trustworthy citizens of the kingdom of God who abides by the laws, rules, regulations and policies of the kingdom of God; neither will He entrust anyone who has shown themselves unfaithful with kingdom power and kingdom glory.

A person who has kingdom power is a person who has been faithful in living under the rule of God, which is what the kingdom of God is all about – it is the rule of God or God's way of doing things. This means we have to renew our minds to be able to live in the kingdom. The kingdom of God is not the Church – the Church is the place where you get taught, trained, equipped, developed and empowered concerning the things pertaining to the kingdom of God to be able to enter God's way of doing things. It is impossible for a person with an unrenewed mind to live in the kingdom. You see, Isaiah 55 clearly says to us that our thoughts are not God's thoughts nor are our way God's ways. Our human thinking is very, very low in comparison with God's thoughts, which is as high as the heaven is above the earth. Much rethinking work needs to be done to narrow this vast gap and to upgrade our minds. Lower thinking produces a lower kind of life; higher thoughts create a higher kind of life. That is what Jesus meant when He said; repent for the kingdom of God is at hand. Repent means to change the way we think.

People in the world are not obligated to pay another 10% of their income after their tax deduction to any organization. Yet, kingdom citizens are required to give 10% and above and beyond 10% of their income after their tax deduction to the Church for the work of the ministry. Just this one kingdom rule proves to everyone that the kingdom of God is a reality of another Government that looks very well after His people, because even though we give more away than anyone outside the kingdom, we still have money left over after the end of the month. People generally have more month left than money. The principle of tithing is a wonder.

I love the words of king David, who said, Thy precepts or principles give life; therefore, we can conclude by saying that the abundant life that Jesus have come to give us is locked up in kingdom principles. I hereby encourage you the reader to search for kingdom principles like a man would seek for a treasure. Buy the truth and sell it not and live by it all the time. Become a respectful citizen of the kingdom of God and the King will entrust you with His power, which is an ability to make great things happen in your life, the people around you, and the world at large. Those of us who are living a life of power must remain faithful with the power that has been entrusted to us. Always keep in mind that we have been given power to make things happen for others. **Look not every man on his own things, but every man also on the things of others** (Phil 2:4). It is far more blessed to give than to receive – we go up when we reach down to others. Our greatest assets in life are our love of serving and our gratitude attitude for getting an opportunity to serve humanity.

The time has come for us to be glorified – whom He justifies, He also glorifies. The anointing removes burdens and destroys yokes; it cannot change and transform the world. We need the glory to change and transform the world and make it a better place for everyone. Serving as many people as possible with the kingdom power that has been entrusted to us is what gives us capacity to carry the weight of God's glory. Remember the words of our Lord Jesus Christ who said that, whosoever serves others wholeheartedly will become great in His kingdom – greatness does not come without glory. Get ready for glory…

Chapter 14

LIVING FRUITFUL LIVES

We read in John 15: 8 that our fruitfulness brings glory to the Father. It is not all our Church activities and religious activities that bring glory to the Father. **Herein is my Father glorified, that ye bear much fruit; so shall ye be my disciples** (John 15:8). A practical example is a tree, since God likens us to trees - He calls us trees of righteousness. A tree can't bear fruit, unless it is rooted and grounded in the depth of the earth, which is the life source of the tree. In the same way, we can't bear fruit unless we are rooted and grounded in God, who is our life Source. **Abide in me, and I in you. As the branch cannot bear fruit of itself, except it abide in the vine; no more can ye, except ye abide in me. I am the vine, ye *are* the branches: He that abides in Me, and I in him, the same brings forth much fruit: for without Me ye can do nothing** (John 15:4-5).

Fruitfulness is also the starting place of our Kingdom Assignment. This implies that we can't do kingdom business unless we are fruitful. This is how our kingdom assignment looks like:

- Be fruitful,
- and multiply,
- and replenish the earth,
- and subdue it:

- **and have dominion over the fish of the sea, and over the fowl of the air, and over every living thing that moves upon the earth** (Genesis 1:28).

These are also stages in our kingdom assignment. I can still remember the day when I have entered the first stage of my kingdom assignment, which is fruitfulness. So many doors opened for me and many opportunities came to me, because things really get added unto us when we seek the kingdom of God first. Those days are still very fresh in my mind – my entire life changed for the good. I can also remember the day I have entered into a stage of multiplication. I am now surrounded by many competent leaders, teams and workers, because I have multiplied myself faithfully over the many years. Our lives and ministry are now well structured to enter into the next stage, which is to replenish the earth to bring kingdom of God influences into the world. This kingdom stuff my friend is so real; it is more real than the breath we breathe. I don't know why we have put off the reality of the kingdom of God on earth for another Age to come. God is so good to us; He gives us the taste of the power of the Age to come. **And have tasted the good word of God, and the works of power of the age to come – Hebrew 6: 5** (Darby)

We are called to be fruitful. It is only when a tree bears fruit that it can multiply itself. Each progressive part of our assignment is a higher level of our kingdom assignment, with fruitfulness being the basis or foundation of our kingdom assignment. All the other aspects of our assignment become easier the more fruitful we become. Answered prayers are also a by-product of a fruitful life. This simply means that God becomes an active partner to those who live fruitful lives. **Ye had not chosen me, but I have chosen you, and ordained you, that ye should go and bring forth fruit, and *that* your fruit should remain: that whatsoever ye shall ask of the Father in my name, he may give it you** (John 15:16). The whole of the Universe will begin to cooperate with us when our desire and God's desire become the same. It was and is the Father's desire for us to represent Him in the earth by carrying out our kingdom assignment.

The ultimate aim of spirituality is to learn to co-operate with God and to allow the Divine will to influence our human will, until the Divine will and our will become one. **For as many as are led by the Spirit of God, they are the sons of God** (Romans 8:14). This is what the journey from the outer courts into the Holy place and into the Most Holy place is all about. All these three dimensions represent the three dimensions of who Jesus is: Jesus is the Christ and He is Lord over everything. By traveling this journey we get to know Him, and by getting to know Him we get to know who we are, because as He is, so are we in this world. **However, the people that do know their God shall be strong, and do exploit** (Daniel 11:32). It is Jesus, who came to show us the Father. Our relationship with Him is the place where fruitfulness starts, and fruitfulness is the starting place of our kingdom assignment. It is all about the King and His Kingdom on the earth.

FRUITFULLNESS IS A TWO-FOLD CONCEPT

Fruitfulness is based on being and doing. It is very interesting to note that God said **be** fruitful and all the other aspects of our kingdom assignment are what we should **do**. *Doing* is a natural outflow of *being,* and *having* is a mere result of the two combined. We are human beings not human doings. Much of the trouble in the world is because people has made the acquisition of stuff their main focus, and this drive them to do certain things to get what they want, instead of focusing on becoming. However, people who are kingdom minded seek the kingdom first, and then all things get added unto them, without them having to run after it (Matt 6: 33). Life is really supposed to be that easy, allowing us to experience sweatless victory. The deeper we travel within the further we go can in life. **Neither**

shall they say, Lo here! or, lo there! for, behold, the kingdom of God is within you (Luke 17:21).

Being (character) is about growing in the fruit of the Spirit. **Even so, the fruit of the Spirit is love, joy, peace, longsuffering, gentleness, goodness, faith, Meekness, temperance: against such there is no law** (Gal 5:22-23). These qualities (fruit of the Spirit) grow in us as we develop an intimate relationship with the Holy Spirit and learn to walk in the Spirit, so that we do not fulfil the lust of the flesh.

- Love,
- Joy,
- Peace,
- Longsuffering,
- Gentleness,
- Goodness,
- Faith,
- Meekness,
- Temperance.

Doing is about competence, potential and our abilities that we have grown through our life experiences, by developing our talents, gifts, life skills, and through equipping, education, training, and development. There are three sets of gifts for those who are called to the five fold ministry and two sets of gifts for those who have not been called to the five fold ministry. Nevertheless, we are all called to do the work of the ministry as ministers of reconciliation. We should all discover our place of grace and giftedness by learning how to flow with the gifts that we have so freely received. In this way, we will become fruitful as we learn to serve each other faithfully with our gifts, talents and abilities.

9 GIFTS OF THE HOLY SPIRIT - 1 COR 12: 8-10
1. Word of wisdom
2. Word of knowledge
3. The gift of faith
4. Gifts of healing
5. The working of miracles
6. Prophecy
7. Discerning of spirits
8. Diverse kinds of tongues
9. Interpretation of tongues

7 MOTIVATIONAL GIFTS - ROMANS 12: 6-8
1. Prophecy
2. Serving
3. Teaching
4. Exhortation
5. Giving
6. Leadership
7. Mercy

5 FOLD MINISTRY GIFTS - EPHESIANS 4: 11
1. Apostle
2. Prophet
3. Evangelist
4. Pastor
5. Teacher

OTHER THINGS THAT CAN MAKE US BECOME FRUITFUL:

Discipling is our secondary assignment, which is an apostolic assignment. It is this secondary assignment that prepares and equips us for our kingdom assignment. It is very important that each believer should be discipled and also to learn the art of discipling others. This is a very sure way of becoming fruitful and productive in our communities and society.

Teach others what you have learned. This reinforces what we have learned, and it gives us the opportunity to sow our knowledge, so that we can reap more. **And the things that thou hast heard of me among many witnesses, the same commit thou to faithful men, who shall be able to teach others also** (2Timothy 2:2). What we teach others become a natural part of us.

Becoming a doer of the Word – so many of us hear the Word of God and never get to a place of doing the Word. This is so evident by the fact that so many believers do not live a blessed life. It is a doer of the Word that gets blessed in whatever they do (James 1: 25). A blessed man or woman is a fruitful man or woman. We need to narrow the gap between hearing and doing. It is within the gap between hearing and doing that deception slips in. **But be ye doers of the word, and not hearers only, deceiving your own selves James 1:22.** I disagree that knowledge is power, because power is the ability to make things happen. Knowing something does not make that thing happen. Knowing without doing is equal to not knowing. Knowledge is potential power or dormant power. The potential power imbedded in knowledge gets released when we apply it. Our lives become fruitful when we apply the Word in our lives.

Learning how to walk in love, so that we might become rooted and grounded, and be able to comprehend with all saints what are the breadth, and length, and depth, and height of God's love. This is how we would come to know the love of Christ, which passes knowledge, that we might be filled with all the fullness of God. The love of God is a force for good; it's the thing that would make us become extremely productive and fruitful in this world, especially when our love becomes perfected and there is no more fear in us (1John 4: 18).

The love of God that has been shed abroad in our hearts should be reflected in its outward appearances. This is how perfect love looks like (1Cor 13: 7-8):

- Love suffers long;
- Love is kind;
- Love envies not;
- Love vaunts not itself;
- Love is not puffed up;
- Doth not behave itself unseemly;
- Seeks not her own;
- Is not easily provoked;
- thinks no evil;
- Rejoices not in iniquity, but rejoices in the truth;
- Bears all things;
- Believes all things;
- Hopes all things;
- Endures all things;
- Love never fails.

Develop your faith; the kind of faith that goes far beyond mere believing. Faith is substance that is made up of many things and these things must be added to our faith, which makes a person become weighty. Let's look at the faith additives that we need to add to our faith to make us become fruitful.

See 2Peter 1: 5-6

- Virtue
- Knowledge
- Temperance
- Patience
- Godliness
- Brotherly kindness
- Charity / love

2Peter 1:8 says this to us: **For if these things be in you, and abound, they make you that ye shall neither be barren nor**

unfruitful in the knowledge of our Lord Jesus Christ. Faith, virtue, knowledge, temperance, patience, godliness, brotherly kindness and love make us become fruitful. These qualities are necessary for us to be effective and efficient in our kingdom assignment. Kingdom business is about taking more and more grounds for the kingdom of God on earth, especially in influential places in the world.

My dear friend, fruitfulness makes life become so easy and effortless. I trust that by now it is common sense that an established prayer life, daily Bible reading, studying and meditation, praise and worship and such like activities are all necessary aspects of our Christian lives to make us become fruitful human beings. We know this, but I want to add that we should always be mindful not to do these things from our minds, always making sure you make a deep heartfelt connection when you do these things. The entry place for a religious spirit is when we do these things from our minds and think we score points with God when doing it. **Jesus said unto him, Thou shall love the Lord thy God with all thy heart, and with all thy soul, and with all thy mind** (Matthew 22:37). It should become our goal in life that our heart, soul and mind become one and that they should not compete with each other, which is really the root cause for a lack of peace in our lives. Allow your heart to take the lead and let your mind be the tool that carries out the instructions of your heart. Do not use your mind to lead your life; God's life is within your heart. Your heart knows what is right for you in any given situation.

LIFE PROCEEDS FROM THE HEART:
- Proverbs 4:23 Keep thy heart with all diligence; for out of it *are* the issues of life.
- Luke 6:45 A good man out of the good treasure of his heart brings forth that which is good; and an evil man out of the evil treasure of his heart brings forth that which is evil: for of the abundance of the heart his mouth speaks.

Do not settle for anything less than fruitfulness! Go for fruitfulness, go for real life! Pray this prayer of Paul regularly over your life. **For this cause we also, since the day we heard *it*, do not cease to pray for you, and to desire that ye might be filled with the knowledge of his will in all wisdom and spiritual understanding; That ye might walk worthy of the Lord unto all pleasing, being fruitful in every good work, and increasing in the knowledge of God; Strengthened with all might, according to his glorious power, unto all patience and longsuffering with joyfulness; Giving thanks unto the Father, which hath made us meet to be partakers of the inheritance of the saints in light:** (Col 1:9-12)

MORE ABOUT THE AUTHOR:

Born and raised in Uitenhage, South Africa. He is happily married to Yolande Daniels with two boys – Jade and Caleb. Winston Lucien Daniels has committed his life to the reconstruction and transformation of the lives of those regarded by society as failures and discarded people. His success is shown by the number of people and families having moved to the garden town of Uitenhage, following
this vision.

Winston Lucien Daniels is also the Author of the Book "The Making of Kings"and "Achieving maximum benefits through minimum effort". Desiring to make more of his own life, he completed Diplomas in Production Management and Industrial Engineering after starting employment at Volkswagen South Africa (VWSA) in 1987, where he progressed through various job promotions, specializing in the area of workflow improvement. Having resigned from permanent employment in 1999, he was recalled a few months later as a private Consultant, responsible for training and educating of VWSA Employees, Team leaders and Supervisors. During this time, he also travelled extensively to other parts of the country consulting to various companies in the area of teambuilding and efficiency improvement, reducing costs and thus increasing revenue.

While at VWSA, Winston also completed his Pastoral Diploma, after serving as Leader and Trainee Pastor at "His People International Ministry" for a number of years, he was then released to start a ministry in what is now known as House of Alpha & Omega International Ministry.

In 2006 Winston retired from formal employment, which enabled him to dedicate himself to full-time ministry work, and freed him up for International Ministry as well. To this end, he has travelled to Australia on a couple of occassions, Egypt, Nigeria, Uganda, Kenya and Zambia.

Website: www.aomi.co.za

Email: kingdom@aomi.co.za

www.ingramcontent.com/pod-product-compliance
Lightning Source LLC
Chambersburg PA
CBHW031844090426
42741CB00005B/348